Lost Restaurants of OMAHA

Lost Restaurants
OF
OMAHA

KIM REINER

AMERICAN PALATE

Published by American Palate
A Division of The History Press
Charleston, SC
www.historypress.net

Front cover, clockwise from top left: courtesy the Kapoun and Bogatz families; courtesy the Kapoun and Bogatz families; courtesy Nebraska State Historical Society; courtesy the Durham Museum Photo Archive and *Omaha World-Herald*.
Back cover, top: courtesy the Durham Museum Photo Archive.

First published 2017

Manufactured in the United States

ISBN 9781625858689

Library of Congress Control Number: 2017945017

Notice: The information in this book is true and complete to the best of our knowledge. It is offered without guarantee on the part of the author or The History Press. The author and The History Press disclaim all liability in connection with the use of this book.

CONTENTS

CONTENTS

ACKNOWLEDGEMENTS

Thank you to the many people who helped me with my research and image collection, including Amy Mather at the Omaha Public Library; Michael Combs and Brian O'Malley at Metropolitan Community College's Institute for the Culinary Arts; the Nebraska State Historical Museum; the Douglas County Historical Society; the Great Plains Black History Museum; Larry Richling with an incredible trove of Omaha history at Hollywood Candy; Lou Marcuzzo, who brought together a group of highly entertaining friends to reminisce, including Dom DiGiaccomo, John Stella, Dan Dasovich and John Sousa; the Kapoun and Bogatz families, especially Terry, Mert and Marsha; and the whole gang at the Durham Museum, especially Bill Gonzalez at the photo archives. Thank you for sharing your insights, Jeff Camp, Brenda Council, Carol Basonek, Irv and Pauline Froydma, Fred Vacanti, Ben Rothe, Gary Coleman and Alexander Payne.

It was a group effort finding first-person sources, and I have many people to thank for helping in the searching, including Jeff Reiner, Randy Goodwin, Mike DiGiacomo, Mike Fisk, Lisa Trudell, Sarah Backhaus, Leo Biga, Ree Kaneko, Betsye Paragas and John Sullivan. Thank you immensely to the thousands of people involved in Forgotten Omaha—your stories, suggestions and photos helped inspire this book.

I'm especially thankful for my editors, Courtney Brummer-Clark, Kelly Robinson and Ann Herrington. And I'm forever thankful for my husband, Kevin, for his support with photos and editing, as well as talking me off the (figurative) ledge several times during the book-writing process.

And thank you to the folks at The History Press for taking a chance on me, and to Chad Rhoad, for being patient with the photo-gathering process.

INTRODUCTION

I'm a born and raised Omaha girl. It took researching and writing a book to realize how little I knew about the place I call home.

Omaha's historic Old Market was once my home for five years, and never once did I investigate the old buildings around me. I didn't delve into the history of Jobber's Canyon, an old district that would have bumped up to my apartment building had it still existed. If it were still there, I could have looked out my window and seen the brick building that was once occupied by Theodore's Bar and Grill. But it's gone.

And yet, there are buildings that still stand in Omaha that were home to remarkable restaurants. I just never realized it.

I didn't think the beautiful building that housed the Magnolia Hotel was ever anything else, even though it was once the hot spot for fashion, on a street that was supposed to be Omaha's answer to New York's Fifth Avenue. Ladies dining at the Aquila Tea Room would peer through the windows to see models parading around the courtyard in the latest styles.

And never once did I stop to think about the interesting building that has the city's oldest restaurant on the second floor: King Fong's. The Tiffany stained-glass windows hint at the luxurious restaurant that was once there. Café Beautiful, it was called. But they do not tell the tale of Tolf Hanson, who opened the ambitious Café Beautiful, and what became of him after it failed.

I'm glad I took up the task of writing this book or I'd never have known such stories. Of course, my first book wasn't going to be nonfiction. But it turns out that if you give a former reporter an assignment, especially if it involves food and a city she loves, she jumps at the opportunity.

I've only eaten at a handful of the restaurants in this book. I never realized just how connected they were to the fabric of my city and how their stories are part of Omaha's story.

And how does Omaha's story go? The city was founded on July 4, 1854, at a picnic where a few optimistic people looked around at a rather unimpressive collection of buildings and envisioned a grand future. One that involved railroads.

Anticipating a great future, an editor of the *Nebraska Republican* wrote, "We have an abiding faith that if our people prove true to themselves, there is a prosperous future for Omaha." Some of the city's first restaurants, like Calumet Coffee House, succeeded thanks to being located near the station.

Decades later, immigrants poured into Omaha, bringing with them recipes from their homelands. In the 1920s, nearly half of Omaha's population were immigrants and their children. They lived in ethnic neighborhoods throughout downtown and South Omaha, including Little Germany, Little Italy (which was really scattered into three neighborhoods), Little Bohemia and Sheeley Town. And you can bet they opened restaurants, many found in this book, like Italian Gardens and Bohemian Café.

In that first century of existence, Omaha's downtown was the place to be—where everyone traveled to shop, dine and be entertained. But once Omaha built highways, the city limits expanded. And like the trend happening nationwide, the downtown area lost its status as a destination. Restaurants like Rose Lodge, Ross' Steak House and Eli Caniglia's Venice Inn began opening in the newly developed West Omaha area, right around Seventy-Second and Dodge Streets. And the people followed.

Omaha's downtown lost its luster. The Old Market was on the verge of extinction. But then, along came developers with an optimistic vision. The French Café opened, and the Old Market revival began. And so it goes with so many of the restaurants in this book.

You can follow Omaha's development through the stories of restaurants. How did Omahans handle Prohibition (or rather the end of Prohibition) or wartime rations? Read the chapters about Piccolo Pete's, Italian Gardens, Marchio's Italian Café or Hilltop House. Did any restaurants have unfair hiring practices before the civil rights movement? Read about Reed's Ice Cream and how months-long protests and picketing reshaped a company policy in Omaha.

It was not easy narrowing down the list of restaurants to include. Some restaurants were open for decades, serving generations of families, and the choice to include them was easy. Other restaurants I included only lasted a short while, but they had a memorable story that I wanted to share. I hope you enjoy their stories as much as I did.

Chapter 1

MAURER'S

"Each City Has Had Its Famous Places. And Omaha Had Its Maurer's."

The story goes that in the early 1900s, a group of men in Chicago were arguing over a rare wine. Four of the men said it couldn't be bought in the United States. The fifth said he knew one person who would have it. Bets were made, train tickets purchased and the quintet traveled to Omaha that night.

They entered Maurer's restaurant and sat at the grill, and the fifth man asked for the wine. Proprietor Ed Maurer went to the cellar. Minutes later, he returned with three bottles chilled on ice.

Of course, they drank all the wine and left confident that the wine could no longer be had in the United States.

*****

In the 1870s, Omaha was transitioning from a frontier town to a glimmer of what it is today: a metropolitan city full of diverse populations.

A German immigrant named Ed Maurer arrived in Omaha in 1876. Having apprenticed in restaurants in Germany and Switzerland, Maurer decided to open a restaurant in the basement of a building at Thirteenth and Farnam Streets. He moved locations, just slightly, to settle between Twelfth and Thirteenth Streets and Farnam. He lost everything in a fire there.

But he wasn't deterred. The restaurant that helped him make a name for himself in Omaha, Maurer's, opened in 1894 at 1306–8 Farnam Street.

An aerial image of Omaha in 1906. *Courtesy Library of Congress.*

When Maurer opened his first restaurant, Omaha was on the cusp of a population boom. The city population was 16,083 in 1870. Thirty years later, at the height of Maurer's restaurant days, it was 102,555.

Maurer's became a dining institution in Omaha. With Swiss-trained chefs, the finest French and German cuisine was served with impeccable, white-gloved service. Maurer was known for high standards of service, requiring everything to be "just so." Some would say it was very "German."

The restaurant served as a meeting place for prominent local businessmen. Among the regulars were Count Edward Creighton, Colonel Frank Hanlon, Judge James Woolworth, Peter Her and John A. Schenk.

Its cosmopolitan air drew people from beyond Omaha. Business executives from the East Coast would plan one-night layovers in Omaha—even if they had no business in town—just so they could enjoy dinner at Maurer's.

Buffalo Bill was said to dine there when he came to town. Everyone, it seemed, wanted to return to the plush setting of the restaurant with the cloth-covered tables under the crystal chandeliers.

THE DELICACIES AT MAURER'S

At noon, men would gather around the grill of the restaurant to eat cheese and sausage and converse in their native languages. An adjoining café would serve men and women. There was a separate area upstairs for women and children to dine in. Occasionally, "women of standing" who wouldn't otherwise visit a restaurant with a saloon would be escorted to Maurer's.

Maurer rose at 4:00 a.m. every day to be at the market for ingredients. He worked like clockwork, so much so that milkmen could set their watches to him.

On a given night, one could dine on fried oyster, lobster, venison or pheasant, as well as some imported delicacies. In the early days of Maurer's, the restaurant served buffalo tongue. But its true appeal to diners was the Nebraska beef, masterfully prepared by the chef. Maurer was so proud of his steaks that he would bring guests back to the cold locker in the basement and hand-select cuts from the hanging steaks.

The chef at Maurer's would even prepare specialty meats that were occasionally brought in by customers. In May 1912, a government official suggested people try eating sparrow. When asked by the *Evening World-Herald* if he'd consider serving the bird, Chef Huller said he would: "I have heard of people eating rats and cats and other things; I guess sparrows would probably make a great hit if the idea were once started." It's not something restaurants could (or would want to) purchase, but Huller and other chefs said if the customer brought a sparrow in, they'd prepare it for them.

Maurer's saloon had sought-after imported liquors and beers. The variety was immense, and of course, there was beer from his native Germany. He had whiskies, brandy, champagne, wine—everything imaginable that would be banned in Prohibition just a few years later.

Everything about the saloon, like his restaurant, was just so. Maurer insisted on bartenders pouring drinks precisely. Kegs had to stand for a certain time. He brought in a bartender from New York City who was a known master of mixology. His arrival created a stir in Omaha. It was noted that Maurer conducted the liquor sales in conjunction with the food department only to make the whole offering complete. Ordering the perfect French wine to complement a meal elevated the experience.

Gerard Coburn Griswold once wrote, "New York had its Rectors, Sherry's, Shanleys, Martin's, Delmonico's, Jack's Waldorf and many others. There were Marchons, the Pup, and the Poodle Dog of Frisco, Cincinnati's St. Nicholas, the Hofbrau of Portland, Boothby's of Philadelphia, Kinsley's of Chicago, Louisville's Seelbach, Kansas City's Morledge, Leuhrmann's of Memphis and 'Madam's' of New Orleans. Each city has had its famous places.

"And Omaha had its Maurer's."

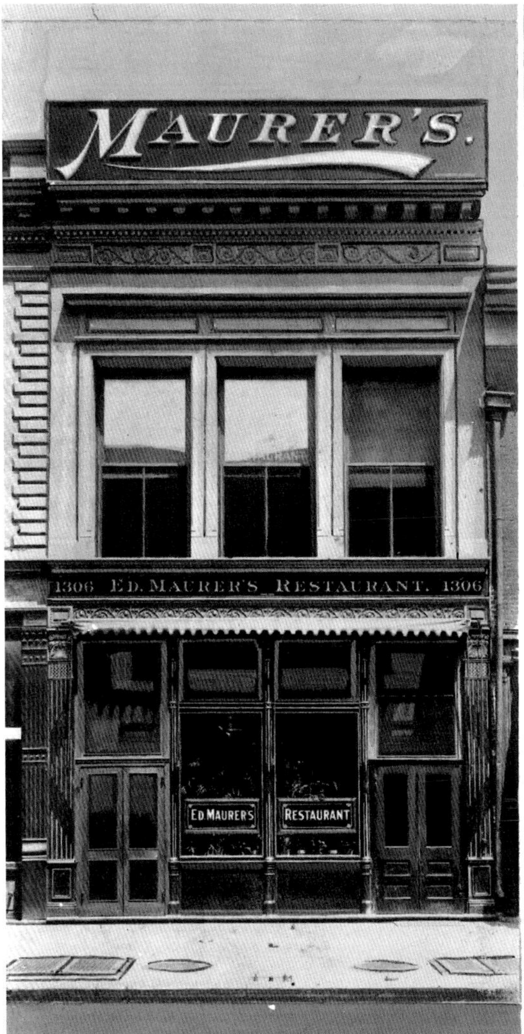

The storefront of Maurer's and a portrait of Ed Maurer. *Courtesy the Durham Photo Archive.*

ATTEMPTED ASSASSINATION AND MINOR CRIMES

In 1888, there was a bit of a stir caused by Maurer's saloon. Maurer was tried in court for obstructing the view into the saloon using curtains, paint and screens. But the jury found Maurer not guilty due to a technical error—the prosecuting attorney failed to have a witness certify that it was Maurer on trial and that he was a dealer of malt and liquor.

In 1909, the restaurant had another brush with the law. Maurer's was fined twenty dollars for having four quail in the chef's possession. They were listed as "rice birds" on the menu.

Maurer's found itself on the front page of the newspaper for an attempted robbery and suspected assassination plot on September 28, 1913. Louis Wesley, a waiter at Maurer's, waited—armed with a revolver—for his boss to open the safe in the basement of the restaurant that morning. A porter surprised Wesley, foiling the robbery. Once police arrived, Wesley stood behind the porter, using him as a human shield. What ensued was a tragedy described by the *Morning World-Herald*: Officer Hiram Cunningham and a bystander were shot, and Wesley was killed. Another assailant, noted by the newspaper as an Italian, escaped.

THE JAZZ ERA LEADS TO MAURER'S END

For twenty-three good years, Maurer's served clientele who lived comfortably and enjoyed fine dining. When Prohibition was established in Nebraska, the tide was changing in Omaha. War raised the cost of food. The jazz era had arrived and changed the entertainment landscape. Maurer decided it was time to close the restaurant. He said he would not turn his establishment into a place for cabaret, and since he believed that was the only thing that was profitable at the time, he closed his doors in November 1917.

When Griswold wrote about the famous restaurants of the United States, he was writing a one-year anniversary letter to the newspaper following the death of Maurer. While it was meant to be a tribute to the fine establishment he ran, it was more so a tribute to Maurer himself. Those who wrote about that period of Omaha would usually mention Maurer's if they mentioned anything at all about restaurants. But to Griswold, there could have been no Maurer's if there hadn't been Maurer.

The building that housed Maurer's is no longer standing. Trees and sidewalks lining the Gene Leahy Mall can be found there.

Chapter 2

CALUMET COFFEE HOUSE AND VIRGINIA CAFÉ

Food Served 'Round the Clock to All Walks of Life

Calumet Coffee House was started by a trio of investors, but its soaring success and eventual downward spiral can be attributed to one man: Tolf Hanson. His spectacular downfall serves as a cautionary tale.

*****

One day at the Old One Minute restaurant in downtown Omaha, two co-workers cooked up the idea for the Calumet Coffee House. Hanson, a Swedish night cook, and Otto Milke, a cashier, dreamed of running a restaurant together. Hanson got his start as a sandwich vendor after immigrating to the United States, and he had the determination to see it through. They just needed a third party to pony up additional start-up money. That's where Emmanuel Johnson came into the picture.

With Johnson, the men opened Calumet on September 23, 1893, at 1413 Douglas Street, where New York Oyster House was previously located. The very first check cashed at the restaurant—for ten cents, paid by Albert Sickel—was saved in a restaurant safe to commemorate the beginning. The check likely covered a large porterhouse steak at the time.

Johnson, considered the "silent partner" in the deal, stayed in the picture only a few years. They were successful years, but Hanson and Milke soon bought out his share of the business.

What exactly the name "Calumet" meant is anyone's guess, and that was probably the point. Johnson had suggested they name the restaurant the Gold Counter, but it was too grandiose for what it truly was. So they settled on Calumet. Hanson and Milke thought the name was intriguing and perhaps people would venture inside to learn what it meant.

ALL WALKS OF LIFE AT CALUMET

From the beginning, the restaurant was a hit. The place was always full from its first day. All walks of life flocked to Calumet—from doctors and lawyers to farmers and cabbies. The *Omaha Bee* once described the scene in 1914: "The head of a large firm finds himself seated beside his humble clerk, each enjoying the meal immensely. The secret of this democratic patronage is a simple one; in each case either the splendid service, the quality of the food or the price is the attraction."

Its reputation spread, drawing visitors from neighboring states and beyond. One newspaper story said it was "no exaggeration to say that it was known from coast to coast." On its best days, it was not uncommon to see people lined up outside to get in.

The restaurant had a horseshoe counter where many would dine and drink. Several notables ate there, including professional boxers Bob Fitzsimmons and Jim Corbett.

It was open twenty-four hours a day. The coffeehouse served a hearty meal for fifteen cents. One could get hot rolls with butter and an order of ham and eggs, bacon and eggs or steak to round out the meal. They exclusively served Courtney's Ankola-brand coffee.

Lunch was hearty. The menu included braised short ribs with horseradish sauce, pot roast with Spanish sauce and huge bowls of oyster stew. In her memoir *Born Rich: A Historical Book of Omaha*, Margaret Patricia Killian recalled that lunchtime was essentially a men's club, with food geared toward a man's substantial appetite. A woman accompanied by a man, she noted, could go there and not be frowned upon, though. Killian recalled one of her favorite specialties, which was simply a large bowl of cold half-and-half served with warm buttered hard rolls.

Calumet held its own against other affordably priced restaurants, including Old One Minute and Charley Bridenbecker's place. The customer was always right, according to Hanson, and everyone who entered was made to feel at home.

Calumet's Dedicated Staff

To keep up with the demand throughout the day, Calumet employed fifteen people in the daytime. At night, a barebones three-man staff worked. Back when Calumet started, only men could be waiters. That soon changed, and some of the longest-employed staff members were women.

Hanson had a way with his staff that created a fierce loyalty. It was said that few worked there for less than twenty years, "unless death cut his career short." If an employee was good enough, Hanson would meet an offer made by another restaurant or raise it in order to keep the employee.

Some of the longtimers included the Swedish-born Carl Moller, who'd worked at Calumet nearly since its inception. Moller spent twenty years there, mostly as second cook and then head cook. There was Anna Wahlstrom, who peeled potatoes for twenty years, and John Fisher, a broiler man for eighteen years. There were other longtimers, including headwaiter Ernest "Ernie" Hodges; Andy Andersen, the doorman; and Charley Anderson, another waiter. Tina Schmidt worked as cashier, leaving Calumet only briefly to work at Hanson's other venture, Café Beautiful, and then returning to Calumet Coffee House after Café Beautiful closed.

Harry Conrad was another longtime employee. He worked the steam table for twenty-four years. His friends once said he sliced enough roast beef to build railroad tracks from Omaha to Chicago. When he was on leave for sixteen weeks, Hanson paid him full wages. On top of that, Hanson once noticed Conrad needed an overcoat and told him to get one and charge it to his account.

During the restaurant workers' strike, his employees said they believed Hanson was with them in spirit, even if he held out against their demands. Policy was dictated by circumstance, not his feelings.

They probably had no idea that at that time, Hanson was dreaming up his next venture.

Hanson's Folly

Hanson was calculating in business. When word spread that a competitor was planning to purchase a vacant storefront nearby, the Calumet owner leased the space for $175 a month and kept it empty. After a few months, he found a clothing store merchant who would lease the space.

Hanson was not content with the success of Calumet. He expanded by opening an annex and private dining room. It meant he now employed one hundred people in a space twice as big as before. There were two meat cooks, four pastry chefs and four men at the steam table.

In 1908, Hanson decided to open Café Beautiful, much to his friends' dismay. They tried to convince him that Calumet was more than enough, but he was confident in his ability to launch a restaurant that could be successful from the start.

Café Beautiful was a bold business venture that was ahead of its time for Omaha. In a year, it sent Hanson into bankruptcy. (See the following chapter for more on Café Beautiful.) Hanson disappeared shortly after the restaurant's demise in June 1909. Hanson's brother-in-law, Sidney Swanson, and Joe Colwell took over Calumet for the creditors and then eventually owned the business themselves.

When Swanson received word that Hanson had committed suicide in New York City, the news was shocking. Family had no reason to suspect he was suicidal and assumed his mysterious departure was intended to be a moneymaking venture.

Hanson's body was returned to Omaha for burial. Calumet closed briefly for his burial. It was one of only three times the restaurant ever closed—and even then, it was only for a few hours. The other closures were in the early 1900s during a strike of restaurant workers and the night of the terrible courthouse riot of 1919.

VIRGINIA CAFÉ AND THE PAYNES

Swanson sold the restaurant to Nicholas Payne in 1920. Payne was already running a successful confectionary business in Council Bluffs, Iowa, with his cousin Fred. The Paynes were a well-known family in the Greek Orthodox Christian community in Omaha.

The cousins remodeled the front of the restaurant and renamed it Virginia Café. They kept the restaurant's efficient waitresses and maintained a very clean restaurant.

Nicholas and Fred kept up Calumet's tradition of remaining open year-round twenty-four hours a day, not even closing on Christmas Day. One time it was forced to close due to smoke and water damage caused by a fire in a nearby building in 1923.

The 1400 block of Douglas Street in 1919, home to Calumet Café. *Courtesy the Durham Photo Archive.*

Virginia Café served a crowd, thanks to a prime spot on the streetcar line and its proximity to large office buildings. The restaurant was contracted to serve enlistees at the nearby recruiting office during World War II, the Korean conflict and the Vietnam War.

Virginia Café grew to a staff of eighty-five and became the largest twenty-four-hour restaurant west of Chicago. The menu was vast and focused on American dishes that changed daily. It was said that they catered to so many different crowds that the restaurant had several menus on hand. It wasn't uncommon to serve thirteen to fifteen selections at lunch in a day.

The food was certainly one reason the Virginia Café lasted for so long, but Nicholas Payne was the other. He greeted his guests and tried every means to make customers feel comfortable. Payne was present nearly all day, coming in at 7:30 a.m., leaving for a two-hour break around lunchtime and returning in the evening for another long shift.

Nicholas Payne's dedication didn't go unnoticed. He was entered into the American Restaurant Magazine's Hall of Fame in 1956 and earned the Omaha Restaurant Association's top honor in 1967, Nebraska Restaurateur of the Year.

Virginia Café earned a good reputation. Local businessmen were the main frequenters there, enjoying daily coffee and happy hours in the restaurant's Redwood Room. Locals working at nearby hotels and theaters would direct visiting national and international celebrities to dine at Virginia Café.

Virginia Café was the Old Market's oldest restaurant when a devastating three-alarm fire occurred on November 9, 1969. Nicholas and his son, George, decided against rebuilding, and the property was sold to Inter City Investment Corporation in 1971. It's now site to W. Dale Clark Library overlooking the Gene Leahy Mall.

Chapter 3

HANSON'S CAFÉ BEAUTIFUL

A Dazzling Restaurant That Was Too Grand to Succeed

Inspired by the ornate cafés in Europe, Tolf Hanson's Café Beautiful was going to be the most magnificent dining establishment ever in Omaha. A $100,000 building remodel—some even put the total cost at close to $175,000—was an astounding amount for the turn of the twentieth century. The new restaurant was to have French chefs who would prepare French cuisine.

Hanson's vision was bold, but it was no match to the reality of 1908 Omaha, and it ultimately led to his ruin. "The life of Tolf Hanson is the story of an ambitious, sensitive, idealist; a man who aspired to the best, of deep sympathies, generous and honest," wrote the *Omaha Daily Bee* following his death a year after his dream was realized.

Hanson was the amiable Swedish co-proprietor of Calumet Coffee House, a successful downtown Omaha coffee shop. Beloved by customers and employees alike, he appeared to be on a course for a comfortable life. But he had a decades-long dream that he had to fulfill first.

Hanson wanted to open a world-class restaurant in Omaha. During a restaurant employee strike, he took off for Europe to wait it out. While there, he solidified his plan. The luxurious cafés overseas were his inspiration.

He told friends about his dream restaurant, and they discouraged him. Hanson figured, Calumet was so successful, how could he fail in this new endeavor?

While still under construction, Hanson pondered the name. He was inclined to call it the Columbia. His friends tried to convince him that his

The dining room of King Fong's with the stained-glass windows from the days of Café Beautiful in the background. *Courtesy Doug Kuony.*

surname should be in the restaurant's name, because "Going to Hanson's" would surely become popular. Ultimately, he called his new venture Café Beautiful.

And it was beautiful. Hanson spent more than $100,000 to bring his dream to life. He hired Chicago architect Meyer J. Sturn to redesign the interior of the Shukert Building at 315 South Sixteenth Street and Omaha-based Fisher & Lawrie to remodel the exterior. Sturn was considered a preeminent architect, and his vision for the interior was to create something that had not been seen even in New York or Chicago yet.

Café Beautiful's Grand Opening

While the soft opening was September 15, 1908, the grand opening was on November 11. Following that first night, a review in the *Morning World-Herald* called it an epicurean paradise: "If Tolf Hanson is proud of the triumph he has achieved and the monument he has built, it can be said that Omaha is also justly proud, and joins hands with the proprietor in general rejoicing."

The opulent exterior made of cream-colored terra cotta was truly a showstopper. The first thing to catch the eye of a pedestrian was the façade, which was an adaptation of the Spanish renaissance style with Flemish Gothic moldings. The ironwork on the façade was treated in a green Tiffany bronze finish. The woodwork was mahogany. The artistic glasswork in front was in an Austrian arts and crafts style and the first of its kind in Omaha. An ornamental marquee projected seven feet from the building.

The entrance to the café was through Atchison revolving doors. To put it into perspective of how advanced those were at the time, the *Omaha Daily Bee* compared it to the motorcar of 1909 versus a Roman chariot.

Once inside the restaurant, the next stunning sight was the Italian Carrara marble stairway to the second floor. It had antique wrought-iron rails and newel posts and a landing large enough to hold an orchestra, as well as the $5,000 Wurlitzer PianOrchestra. The first-floor décor was described as a German adaptation of L'Art Nouveau. The kitchen was located on the first floor, along with the main dining room. The kitchen was state-of-the-art for its time and equipped by Milton Rogers & Sons.

There were four additional floors, if you count the basement, which could be accessed by stairs from the sidewalk. In the basement, customers found the beautiful lunchroom, with natural oak finishing and glazed tiles on the floors, walls and ceiling. Advertisements boasted it was the "most attractive

A view of the stained-glass windows of King Fong Café, which are one of the few things remaining from Hanson's Café Beautiful. *Courtesy Doug Kuony.*

lunch room in Omaha." The basement was also used for wine storage and had refrigerators for meat.

The second floor had a service room for the upstairs restaurant and banquet halls. The ladies dined on that floor. The cozy room was designed in the Empire style, with cream-colored woodwork and chairs and lamp bases in antique green. The walls and ceilings were cream colored as well, and the ceiling had ornamental tiles. The large, ornamental oval dome above the stairwell was a key feature.

The third floor had storerooms, vegetable preparation rooms, dishwashing rooms and the bakery. The fourth floor had what they called the ventilation plant, essentially a place to pipe air into and out of the building. The *Omaha Daily Bee* described the exhaust fans on the fourth floor as capable of removing all malodorous air from the building.

Everything about the restaurant was designed to impress. Fixtures were imported, and the employees were semi-imported. Hanson brought in French waiters and chefs from New York to complete the atmosphere, advertising the skill of the white waiters. But instead of impressing, it put off people.

"The high toned French waiters and the high toned French dishes concocted by the high toned French chefs didn't make a hit," one critic wrote.

A QUICK END TO A DREAM

In less than a year, it was clear the restaurant was a losing venture. Much of the problem had to do with the lease, which the *Omaha Daily Bee* called a monumental mistake. Hanson was to pay a $10,000 annual rent for ten years, after which the building and all improvements went back to G.E. Shukert. It was a business impossibility. Every day was said to add to the debt, with income below $1,000 even on the best days. Hanson's payroll and expenses far exceeded that.

Some said it was a café built for Omaha ahead of its time—about twenty-five to fifty years ahead of its time. If clientele from Calumet were tempted to follow Hanson over to Café Beautiful, they encountered prices far exceeding what they were used to.

In a bittersweet turn of fortune, a man who had started out selling sandwiches was beaten by his pride. He disappeared on June 30, 1909, following Café Beautiful's financial failure, leaving behind the still-thriving

The dining room at King Fong Café. *Courtesy Doug Kuony.*

Calumet. He headed to New York City in search of funding; his family believed he was straightening out his business affairs. A local newspaper would report updates on his whereabouts by way of friends who'd seen him. He bragged about how well his business was doing and told one friend he was making $4,000 a month.

Certainly that would have been news to his creditors, who had taken over Café Beautiful in July 1909. Hanson was liable for about $150,000, but his assets appeared to be no more than $40,000. Creditors had to cover a loss of more than $100,000.

About two months after Hanson's disappearance, word was sent over the wire on September 1, 1909, that he had committed suicide in New York City. It was a shock to his wife, Jennie, and his mother. One newspaper reported his family believed it was accidental.

Hanson's body was returned to Omaha for burial. Calumet suspended service for a half hour so friends, employees and patrons could grieve.

Shortly after Café Beautiful closed, Robertson's Restaurant moved into the location for about ten years. The space has been occupied since the 1920s by King Fong Café, considered Omaha's oldest Chinese restaurant. Its extensive menu has eight pages of entrées and sides. The owners were proud of the food and appearance and expressed as much in a note in an early menu: "The camphor wood carvings, the hand-carved teak-wood chairs, the elaborate silk embroideries, the hand-carved tables and other notable features that have been imported from the Flowery Kingdom at great expense."

King Fong Café closed for remodeling in March 2016. It had not reopened at the time of this printing.

Chapter 4

EMPRESS GARDENS

Luxury Dining at Popular Prices

In the early twentieth century, Omaha had a few adventurous restaurateurs who attempted to bring a new grand concept to the city's dining scene. In similar fashion as Café Beautiful, Empress Gardens restaurant was a short-lived, extravagant addition to downtown Omaha.

In 1913, A. LeMarquand, W.S. Aargaard Jr. and Frank Harris opened Empress Gardens, a restaurant in the large basement of Empress Theater at 1414 Harney Street. The owners outfitted it for $90,000, including a bakery and a deli slicer, and in exchange, they enjoyed a fifteen-year free lease agreement. Unfortunately, it was needed. The restaurant was only in business for a few months before trouble began.

The problem with Empress Gardens was that its mode of business was unsustainable. As ads claimed, it offered a luxury dining experience at popular prices. It claimed to serve more than eight thousand customers in a week, but with the low prices, they couldn't keep the business afloat.

And it was a luxurious restaurant. It had a beautiful soda fountain under the stairs and a balcony that overlooked the first-floor dining room. Diners sat in Austrian bentwood chairs, while plants and ferns were placed between tables to create intimacy. There were softly glowing lights throughout, and posts and pillars were wrapped in lattice. Oil paintings hung from the walls on the main floor and mezzanine level. A large glass window separated the dining room from the kitchen so patrons could watch food being prepared in the all-aluminum kitchen.

Left: A postcard of the Empress Theater at night. Empress Gardens was in the basement of the Empress Theater. *Author's collection.*

Below: The staircase in the Empress Gardens dining room in 1917. *Courtesy the Durham Photo Archive.*

On the south end of the mezzanine floor, a space was created for cabaret performers. Two baby grand pianos were in place to accompany performers. One of the acts that performed there was the Royal Hawaiian Harmonists.

Standing Out in the Omaha Dining Scene

Breakfast was short-order, but things changed for lunch and dinner service. Empress Gardens offered "table d'hôte," or prix fixe menus. When most restaurants were serving food cafeteria style, Empress Gardens tried to be different: servers would push teacarts through the aisles. For thirty-five cents, customers could get a lunch of cream of celery soup with German salami sausage and smoked marinated herring, roast pork loin, applesauce, peas in butter, brown potatoes and assorted French pastries. Diners could also get coffee, tea or a bottle of milk.

Dinner, served from 5:00 to 8:00 p.m., was fifty cents and would have looked something like this: consommé tapioca *crecy* (essentially, a French style of soup), crab flake mayonnaise, stuffed olives, roast chicken, potatoes duchess, Venetian vanilla ice cream and Sunshine Cake. Between meals, diners could stop in for the buffet, which sometimes would serve oysters, lobster, salads, sandwiches, deli meats and pastries. Empress Gardens had a deli, as well, where customers could purchase lunches and meats to take home.

Its location drew in the theater crowd. Because of this, it was the site of an elaborate party for motion picture executives. The party made the news, but not for a good reason. In April 1914, the managers and owners of motion picture theaters at the Empress Gardens wanted to host a formal affair. Mayor James C. Dahlman spoke that night. Food was fifty cents a plate, and each attendee got a bottle of beer. The Empress wasn't known for serving alcohol, but the manager of the theater, Harris—who was co-owner of the restaurant—was assured by the mayor and chief of police that this was custom for those types of party, so they abided.

At some point in the night, three cases of beer were stolen. The party allegedly ended at 2:00 a.m., but that would prove not to be the case. A police report from that night stated a seventeen-year-old boy got drunk at the party. Harris suggested he left sober and continued to party with the stolen beer until he made his way home at 3:45 a.m. It was a bit of a scandal. The head usher from the theater was charged with aiding and abetting the delinquency of a minor. His $500 bond was paid by his employers.

A mere few days later, the restaurant was in the news again. The Empress Gardens was in financial trouble. Starland Limited, the lessor of the premise and proprietor of the theater, complained it was owed more than $20,000. Other businesses complained they hadn't been paid for signs, supplies and other services. In late April 1914, the restaurant was put in the hands of a receiver. Its only assets were the equipment and its fifteen-year lease. The restaurant eventually went bankrupt.

It closed in September 1914. Most items from Empress Gardens were auctioned off.

EMPRESS GARDENS REVIVAL

On May 1, 1917, P.H. Philpin reopened the restaurant under the same name. He still billed it as Omaha's finest restaurant but added "amusement center" to its description. Philpin advertised the restaurant as a "Refined Resort for Cultured People." The restaurant now had a $10,000 pipe organ, sophisticated decor and a full entertainment schedule.

In the first week of business, the restaurant featured a variety of entertainment, including Omaha's popular female impersonator Walter Adams. Additional performers included the classical dancer Miss Patsy, assisted by J. Harrold Williams, and child entertainers Thelma Wolpa and Tommy Bonny, who had just presented a song-and-dance show at the Orpheum Theater. During the week, the live entertainment varied from vaudeville and dancers to vocalists. On Sundays, the music was semi-sacred and patriotic—and certainly no dancing. Under new ownership, Sunday table d'hôte dinners were one dollar.

The revival of Empress Gardens lasted longer than the original, but it met an unfortunate fate. A fire in June 1918 shut down the restaurant.

Two years later, a new version of Empress Gardens emerged. This time, it was called the Empress Rustic Garden. The interior was completely remodeled.

By day, it was a charming tearoom and ice cream parlor. It was considered more sophisticated than the run-of-the-mill ice cream parlor, with lavish decor and impressive china. By night, it was the biggest place to dance in Omaha.

The owner, Wilfred Ledoux, created themed nights to bring in crowds. There was a Valentine's Day dance and one for St. Patrick's Day, and in December, Santa was spotted there handing out gifts.

A year into business, Empress Rustic Gardens was already known for having a few disturbances. On New Year's Eve 1920, a young man was shot. About a week later, a twenty-year-old shopgirl was arrested for wearing a dress stolen from Brandeis. There was a car stolen from in front of the building in February.

The Empress Rustic Gardens was open for about seven years before it had its last dance. On July 11, 1927, the fixtures were all auctioned off. Immense crowds gathered for the auction, hoping to walk away with some of the beautiful silver, glassware and china.

The building was razed in 1929.

Chapter 5

THEODORE'S BAR AND GRILL

The Jobbers Canyon Grill That Lived On Even after the End of Jobbers Canyon

Theodore's Bar and Grill was one of the restaurants and bars that thrived in Jobbers Canyon for decades. It wasn't particularly known for its food or atmosphere; it was its clientele and kind owner that made it stand out from other lost restaurants of Omaha.

Jobbers Canyon was a downtown district of warehouses and buildings, and the employees of the area were working-class laborers. When an Italian immigrant, Theodore Parachini Sr., opened the restaurant at 601 South Tenth Street in 1918, horses were still used to transport goods through downtown Omaha. It was called Theodore's Place in the beginning.

Theodore's was a welcoming restaurant to the blue-collar workers of Jobbers. Whether it was a noontime lunch or a cold beer at the end of a workday, they found it at Theodore's. They came for the hot roast beef sandwich or chili or to cash a paycheck. The restaurant wasn't very large. There were about ten stools at the bar and a handful of booths, plus a long corridor.

The restaurant stayed in the family when Theodore "Ted" Parachini Jr. assumed ownership after his father passed away. At the time, the younger Parachini was still a student at Creighton University, but he'd already been working at the restaurant since his early teens.

Carol Bosanek, the daughter of Parachini Jr., recalled the restaurant was one of many in Jobbers Canyon, but her father distinguished himself through his kindness. Parachini Jr. was an amiable man and ran a good business for decades. He had a reputation for helping anyone who needed it.

Left: Exterior of Theodore's Place. *Courtesy Carol Bosanek.*

Below: Theodore's Place in the 1930s. *Courtesy Carol Bosanek.*

Theodore "Ted" Parachini Jr., *left*, with two other bartenders at Theodore's Bar and Grill on April 29, 1943. *Courtesy Carol Bosanek.*

While Bosanek and her sister weren't allowed to spend much time in the restaurant, except to help with spring cleaning, she recalled the time the Budweiser Clydesdales were in town and made a stop at the distributor near Theodore's. Her whole family went to Jobbers Canyon that day to see them.

When Parachini Jr. retired in 1978, the restaurant transferred hands again. While a couple of sons-in-law had worked at the restaurant for a time, no one in the Parachini family was willing to take over. The sons of a longtime cook at the restaurant, Ace Lalley, bought the restaurant. One of those sons, Tom Lalley, had been co-owner with his brother for some time when he became the sole owner. The change in ownership wasn't a disappointment to Parachini Jr. He admitted to family that running a restaurant wasn't a fun business to be in.

Tom Lalley had a run-in with the law in his younger days, but under his leadership, the restaurant weathered the razing of its original home, relocation and eventual real estate negotiations of its second home.

The End of Jobbers Canyon

Theodore's stayed in its original location in Jobbers Canyon for more than seventy years. During that time, it never drew much attention to itself, besides winning an odd readers' poll here and there. The *Observer* had a readers' poll in 1983, and Theodore's won second place for live entertainment…except there was never live music performed there. A reporter for the *Omaha World-Herald* quipped that Theodore's didn't have live entertainment "except for the customers, who are, I have to admit, often quite entertaining."

True, there were some regulars who were quite memorable. One of the daughters of the younger Theodore recalled some characters, like a man named Montana. With the new owners, though, came a new sort of clientele, and the restaurant wasn't quite the same again.

In the late 1980s, the home of Theodore's Bar and Grill and surrounding businesses faced an ultimatum. The corporate giant ConAgra wanted a new headquarters, and Jobbers Canyon was in its sights. Throughout lengthy negotiations, there was a lot of uncertainty if a deal could be reached. The corporation needed a sizeable amount of land to build its campus.

In early January 1988, a deal was reached. The night the deal was struck to tear down Jobbers Canyon, the men at the bargaining table ate hamburgers brought in from Theodore's, one of the businesses whose building would eventually be razed. Part of the agreement called for the city to participate in the "friendly" condemnation of the seven Jobbers Canyon properties. This allowed for the warehouse owners to avoid paying capital gains taxes. None of the owners protested, and eventually, Jobbers Canyon was no more.

Theodore's Bar and Grill relocated to 4684 Leavenworth Street after the ConAgra riverfront development started in 1990. It carried on in its new location for six more years before real estate developers once again eyed its neighborhood and deemed it ready for redevelopment.

The restaurant was sold along with neighboring properties to developer Real Estate Brokerage Company to make a Quik Trip convenience store. Theodore's closed in September 1996.

Chapter 6

BOHEMIAN CAFÉ

Where Everyone Was Czech for the Day, Because That's How Long the Dumplings Stayed with You

In the early 1900s, Bohemian Café was one of the big three Czech institutions in a downtown neighborhood full of Eastern European immigrants. Over time, its popularity grew, and it began to attract non-Czechs. By the time the restaurant closed in 2016, it was one of Omaha's longest-running restaurants, serving up dumplings and other hearty old-world fare for more than ninety-two years.

According to a 1988 review in the *Omaha World-Herald*, "They say that on St. Patrick's Day, everyone is Irish. But every day of the year, anyone who visits the Bohemian Café is bound to feel at least a little bit Czech."

The little neighborhood around Thirteenth and William Streets used to be the center of "Novy Svet," or the New World, as it was known to Omaha's Czech community. Immigrants new to America could get all their needs met in this Little Bohemia. Czech-owned businesses were all within a few blocks—groceries, a barber, a shoe store, the Prague Hotel. There was St. Wenceslaus Catholic Church and Sokol Hall, where dances, gymnastic tournaments and the Bohemian Grape Harvest festival were held. *Narodni Pokrok*, the Czech-language newspaper, was published in the neighborhood.

At the start of the twentieth century, the area felt very much like a Bohemian town. Immigrants conversed in their native language, and some dressed in old-world clothing. The second generation had begun to learn English and integrate into Omaha life, but not the older generation.

The Reverend Anthony Tuma served the Omaha Czech Catholic community for decades and described how the 1930s were on Thirteenth

Street to the *Omaha World-Herald*: "There was everything you could want—shoes, clothing, bakeries, sausages....Czech was still spoken in the stores and on the street. We had our own newspaper. [Church] services were largely in Czech."

There were a handful of restaurants, too, including what would become Bohemian Café. Louie Macala, a Czech immigrant, opened a little stand in 1925 at the Kopecky Hotel at 1431 South Thirteenth Streeth, where he sold soft drinks and snacks to Czech-Americans. Sometime around 1933, he moved into the Hinky Dinky store at 1236 South Thirteenth and ran his restaurant known as Louie Macala Restaurant. In 1935, its name changed to Bohemian Café.

THE GRAND DAYS OF THE BOHEMIAN CAFÉ

The restaurant grew in popularity in the 1950s, thanks largely to the new owners, Josef and Ann Libor. The couple were Czech immigrants who came to the United States as children. Josef had left Prague in advance of the Communist takeover. In 1948, they bought the restaurant from Macala, who stayed on as chef. The combination of the new owners and Macala's menu was a recipe for success.

The *Omaha World-Herald* described a typical Sunday night at the restaurant in the late 1940s:

> *The eating is done. The air is thick with cigar and pipe smoke from the men sitting at the wooden tables playing pinochle and sipping a slivovitz or a cold Pilsner Urquell. At other tables, women gather to gossip. Children play on the wooden floor, scurrying after toys. Waitresses in red peasant-style uniforms move about, cleaning up the remains of duck bones and the dollops of dumplings and gravy left unfinished. Over in the corner is Josef Libor at the piano. Once a concert musician, the gregarious Libor is playing polkas and waltzes and an occasional composition by Antonin Dvorak, the famous Czech composer.*

Even into the 1950s, Josef would sit at the keyboard and an instant Czech party would begin.

Occasionally, polka bands passing through town would stop at the restaurant for a meal. Those meals were often followed by lively impromptu concerts, much to the delight of customers and staff.

Friends of the Libors gather inside at the first location of Bohemian Café with Ann, *second from left*, and Josef Libor, *second from right. Courtesy the Kapoun and Bogatz families.*

The restaurant was moved again in 1959, just a block over to 1406 South Thirteenth Street. The move changed the look of the restaurant to what most people remember now. Some called the new look kitschy or reminiscent of a gingerbread house. Regardless, it attracted its fans and newcomers alike.

Left: Josef and Ann Libor, *on the right*, in front of the Bohemian Café when it was located at 1236 South Thirteenth. *Courtesy the Kapoun and Bogatz families.*

Below: Josef Libor, *seated in front*, and Ann Libor, *back row on the right*, with some of the waitresses at Bohemian Café. *Courtesy the Kapoun and Bogatz families.*

Ann Libor in the dining room of Bohemian Café. *Courtesy the Kapoun and Bogatz families.*

The bar at the Bohemian Café in the late 1950s. *Courtesy the Kapoun and Bogatz families.*

Bohemian Café's exterior had an arched doorway and windows framed by ceramic tiles with colorful floral designs. The sign out front was a chance for the owners to announce a love for their culture. In the 1970s and '80s, it read what many Czechs had been saying of their native country: "Russians, get out of Czechoslovakia!" In the restaurant's final years, it simply read "*Vitame Vas*" ("We Welcome You").

The interior was comfortable, with a familiar feeling to it. There was highly polished woodwork, carpeting and hanging baskets filled with fake flowers. Pictures of painted Czech countryside scenes hung on the walls. Collections of European glassware and a case of Jim Beam decanters shaped like women in traditional costumes rounded out the décor.

"The Bohemian Café has a niche in the Omaha restaurant scene, with few competitors," wrote an *Omaha World-Herald* reviewer in 1992. "It wisely stays with what has kept customers coming back, year after year. A fine lunch spot, it offers hearty dinners at reasonable prices—and a touch of Old World cuisine and hospitality."

FIVE MILLION DUMPLINGS SOLD

When the Libors' daughter, Mert Kapoun, took over the restaurant with her husband, Bob, in 1966, few things changed. In fact, the restaurant stayed in her family until the end. Generations of the Kapoun family lived in the apartment above the restaurant. "This was the hub of our family," said Mert's son, Terry, who would eventually be the last Kapoun to own the restaurant. "We got to see Mom every day."

The dishes were close to what Ann and Josef, known as "Babi" and "Deda" to the family, had served for twenty years. To prepare the long-simmered food, the chef usually was up before dawn. Ron Kapoun filled that role starting in 1969 until the restaurant's end thirty-seven years later.

The menu was heavy on the Eastern European fare, with a light sprinkling of more Americanized items. Diners got a hearty meal for not a lot of money. There was liver dumpling soup, breaded sweetbreads, Polish sausage and plum dumplings. Specialties included *svickova*, a Czech-style sauerbraten or slices of marinated beef; *jaeger schnitzel*, veal steaks in wine sauce and mushrooms; *hasenpfeffer*, braised rabbit topped with sour cream gravy; and Czech goulash. Dinner entrées came with a choice of sauerkraut, vegetable or sweet and sour cabbage; choice of Czech dumplings (and they were quite large and topped with a yellow-gray gravy made of beef, pork

Exterior of the Bohemian Café. *Courtesy Kevin Reiner.*

and duck stock); whipped potatoes or French fries; and choice of soups. Rye bread and crackers came out before diners ordered. In 1988, that would cost about $5.50.

One of the most popular entrées, especially with the older Czech customers, was the roast duck. An *Omaha World-Herald* reviewer in 1988 described it as "both unusual and reminiscent of something your mother would serve you." In later years, goulash and *svickova* were requested more.

In the early 1990s, the Bohemian Café owners invited the Czech national volleyball team to dinner at the restaurant. The team had a match at Omaha's Civic Auditorium. The players gave Ron Kapoun the ultimate compliment: "Just like Mom used to make."

In a 2013 column in *Saveur* called "Bohemian Rhapsody," Czech native Mila Saskova-Pierce wrote about the café:

> *Its foods—rich duck liver dumpling soup; svickova, sauerbraten enriched with sour cream; sweet and sour cabbage; kolaches, pastries with poppyseed, Bavarian cream, prune, cherry, and other fruit centers—were like the dishes my grandmothers prepared for Sunday family gatherings in Prague, where I grew up. I left there in 1968 when I was 20. But at the Bohemian Café, I felt right back at home.*

Like dining at grandmother's dinner table, the servings were enormous. A restaurant reviewer once likened dining at the Bohemian Café to a meal at grandma's: "And having her keep pushing food at you, even though you couldn't eat another bite without major surgery to expand the stomach." The author of *Omaha Food: Bigger Than Beef* described the portions as "hilariously large." She also said the restaurant's co-owner, Marsha Bogatz, had explained that "if you leave here hungry, we are doing something wrong."

If a customer had room for it, there were drinks and dessert to enjoy too. Drinks included Czech beer Pilsner Urquell and American beers served in chilled mugs. For an after-dinner option, the Kapouns had *slivovitz*, a colorless plum brandy, on the menu, but that was dropped more than a decade before they closed since it was hard to come by. Desserts included *kolacky*, a roll filled with gelatinous fruit, poppy seed or Bavarian cream and powdered sugar; and apple strudel with a pastry crust that was soft and flaky, almost pie-like, with cinnamon-flavored apples and raisins.

It was the dumplings, though, that everyone remembered and returned for. The doughy specialty was even immortalized in the restaurant's jingle:

Dumplings and kraut today
At Bohemian Café
Draft beer is sparkling
Plenty of parking
See you at lunch—OK?

When Terry Kapoun greeted tour groups, he'd let them know they were "honorary Czechs for a day—because that's how long the dumplings stay with you."

Loyalty to the Restaurant

A waitress at Bohemian Café. *Courtesy Lori Mangiameli.*

There was something about the restaurant and the Kapoun family that inspired loyalty among staff and customers alike. It wasn't uncommon for an employee to work at Bohemian Café for decades. Gerry Coufal was a waitress from 1967 until 2016. Lori Mangiameli worked there for forty-two years. Joe Maggio told the *Omaha World-Herald* he'd begun working at the restaurant when he was in junior high and stayed on staff for twenty-seven years. He returned to work there in the restaurant's final months.

The restaurant's clientele was just as loyal. The Czech groups who met in the restaurant's early days continued to meet there, even though most no longer lived in the neighborhood. Some families dined every Easter or Thanksgiving at the restaurant, a tradition that allowed staff to marvel as the families grew in size.

"It started out as a husband and wife coming here, then they had kids and came here and then their grandkids came along, and toward the end, there'd be thirty-five of them," Terry Kapoun recalled how it usually went. "You didn't just *see* them, you got to know the family."

Terry's sister Marsha worked at the restaurant as well and said if she hadn't seen a regular in a while, she'd start to worry. "You do become a family, even with the customers," she said.

In early 2016, the Kapoun family announced the restaurant's last day. There were a couple of reasons for Bohemian Café's end. Kapoun family members were aging, for one thing. Ron Kapoun was ready for retirement after nearly four decades in the kitchen. There was also a drop in business—which became ironic when crowds began to roll in after they announced they would be closing. They shifted to dinner-only hours and maintained steady business until the end.

Those last four months, said Terry Kapoun, were festive like the old days. "Like fifty parties going on at the same time."

Many of the restaurant's most memorable elements could be seen or heard or tasted up until its final days: the red uniforms that resembled traditional costumes, the gravy dumplings, even the polka music, though it was eventually recorded music.

The last dumpling was served on September 24, 2016.

Chapter 7

AQUILA TEA ROOM

The Place Where the Fashionable Dined

Aquila Court was a self-proclaimed Fashion Corner located at 1615 Howard Street. When the building was under construction, ads proclaimed that it was going to turn the nearby Saint Mary's Avenue into Omaha's version of New York's Fifth Avenue. It was the most expensive building built in Omaha in 1923, costing $750,000. It was, according to the developers, the first building to have a commercial courtyard of its kind in the United States. In reality, it drew inspiration from the Italian Gardens of Chicago.

Tenants in the building were carefully screened in order to keep a fashionable appearance and tone. One such tenant who made the cut was Maude Borup, who ran a candy shop and the trendy Aquila Tea Room. Her tearoom opened on May 28, 1924, shortly after Aquila Court opened. It occupied the southwest corner of the first floor.

The building became a high-fashion destination, as the clothing stores put on fashion shows. Models paraded in the latest styles around its beautiful outdoor fountain court. Department stores and clothing boutiques such as Haas Brothers Company Fashion Salons had shows there. The setting was beautiful: rough flagstone with a brook running through the middle.

From Aquila Tea Room's nineteen windows, women at lunch could enjoy a lovely view of the parade in the courtyard. "Watching fashions being modeled while dining on exceptionally well-prepared tea room fare, was something no one living here at that time will ever forget," wrote Margaret Patricia Killian in her memoir.

Left: The courtyard at Aquila Court, now part of the Magnolia Hotel. *Courtesy Tim Trudell.*

Below: A women's group meeting in the courtyard of Aquila Court in 1934. *Courtesy the Durham Museum Photo Archive.*

Exterior of the Aquila Building. *Courtesy Tim Trudell.*

DINING AT AQUILA TEA ROOM

Borup, originally from St. Paul, Minnesota, prepared elaborate plates with artistic garnishes. Luncheon food included smooth cream soups and *consomme Madrilene*, a clear broth flavored with tomatoes and served chilled. There would be crab-stuffed avocado pear salads and deviled crab in shells, as well as the typical hot or cold sandwiches, elevated by exquisite embellishments on the salad plates. There was also a candy shop.

In late December 1932, Borup planned a couple tea dances, advertised as *Tea Dansante*. These afternoon parties included live music by Collegiate Orchestra and refreshments, all included with a cover charge of thirty-five cents.

Several changes to the tearoom occurred in 1934. In the summer, the tearoom boasted an update: air conditioning. That fall, the restaurant began to serve dinners. They became a specialty. The fireplace crackled, and tables were candlelit. A dinner in 1935 cost between eighty cents and one dollar.

The Engagement That Forced Maude out of the Tearoom

Four days after announcing her engagement to Charles T. Kountze, building management announced they'd find a replacement for Borup. She'd get to maintain an advisory role, but the building management wanted to place day-to-day operations in the hands of "some Omaha girl or woman socially prominent."

Borup fired back her response less than a week later. She informed the *Omaha World-Herald* that her approaching marriage would not interfere with managing Aquila Tea Room: "There will be no change in the management of the tea room, because I have no intentions of giving it up."

Ultimately, she did leave the tearoom. First, she moved the candy shop to Seventeenth and Howard Streets on January 1, 1926. By the end of the tearoom's run—closing in September 1937—the Aquila Court owners, Chester A. and Raymond Cook, were managing it.

The Aquila Court building is now part of the Magnolia Hotel chain, housing its only Omaha location. The courtyard is still there and is used for weddings, happy hours and other gatherings for hotel guests.

Chapter 8

REED'S ICE CREAM

Ice Cream Was an Affordable Luxury in Tough Times

The Depression hit hard in Omaha. One would think a new restaurant in 1929 wouldn't stand a chance of surviving, but not all restaurants had the novelty or attraction that Reed's Ice Cream had.

With $18,000 to start a business, Claude Reed was eighteen when he came to Omaha to open a branch of Reed's Ice Cream, a company founded by his father, J.D. Reed, in Des Moines, Iowa. J.D. had been manufacturing ice cream in Iowa since 1901.

Claude Reed opened the Omaha plant at 3106 North Twenty-Fourth Street in 1929 with his business partner, C.F. Becker. The following year, he built ten locations in Omaha. Designed to look like quaint dollhouses, these small bungalows had white siding, green trim and lace curtains. Claude did most of the work, it seemed in the early days—manufacturing, delivering and helping staff the stands.

"Pure sweet cream + sugar + flavor of fruit juices + careful blending" read one 1930 ad explaining the product.

It was a tough sell, at first. Customers were used to hand-packed ice cream that was sold in paper cartons called oyster buckets. Reed's approach was different. Ice cream was sold prepackaged. Reed lost $800 the first year, selling forty thousand gallons of ice cream. By his third year, he turned a profit.

Luxury in Tough Times

Reed's thrived because of one simple thing: it was cheap but felt like a luxury in a time of hardship. Families considered it a night of entertainment to walk to the neighborhood Reed's Ice Cream stand for a nickel cone or dime malt.

Decades later, Claude Reed reflected on the experience of running a business in the 1930s: "Going to Reed's gave you a chance to treat the kids and talk to neighbors. In those days people would rather give up a necessity than a little luxury. They'd cut out some meat and potatoes to buy ice cream."

Families struggling through the Depression would splurge to purchase a gallon of ice cream in any of the twenty flavors for fifty-five cents. A quart was only seventeen cents. Reed's kept the prices low by smart and efficient manufacturing and distribution.

In its heyday after the Great Depression, there were 63 stands in Omaha and Council Bluffs and a total of 117 outlets stretching to Des

The exterior of one of the Reed's Ice Cream locations in 1938. In its heyday following the Great Depression, Reed's Ice Cream had sixty-three locations in Omaha and Council Bluffs. *Courtesy the Durham Museum Photo Archive.*

Exterior shot of a Reed's Ice Cream. *Courtesy Nebraska State Historical Society.*

Moines and St. Louis. In Omaha, at its peak, Reed's served more than 20,000 Omahans a day. More than one million gallons of ice cream were sold in a year, and it grossed $2.5 million annually. There were 250 employees. Claude Reed once said Reed's dispensed 40 percent of the ice cream sold in Omaha.

Folks would reminisce through the years about Reed's. One man told the *Omaha World-Herald* about his recollections of Reed's Ice Cream giveaways in the 1940s over the radio. The announcer would read four questions over the air at 9:15 p.m., five nights a week. To win, you had to write your answers on paper and bring them to one of the Reed locations, where winners were announced at 10:00 p.m. A lot of people always had the correct answers, so they'd place the list in a container and a child would draw the winning entry.

THE CIVIL RIGHTS ERA AND REED'S

Reed's Ice Cream came under scrutiny in the early 1950s for its hiring practices: it refused to hire black employees. At a time before the civil rights movement even began, a group in Omaha wanted to change that. Members of the Omaha DePorres Club along with the *Omaha Star*, Nebraska's first newspaper published by a black woman, fought hard for equal rights, already having led peaceful marches and written pointed editorials aimed at businesses that did not hire black employees, including Omaha's transportation system and Coca-Cola.

Early requests to Reed's Ice Cream to change its hiring practices were followed by a letter published in 1953 in the *Omaha Star* stating:

> *This unfair policy of denying equal job opportunities to Negroes, especially because of your large number of Negro customers has for too long stood in complete violation of the American ideal of equal opportunity....Beginning Monday, January 19, unless we hear from you before then, we will stop supporting your unfair policy by not buying Reed's ice cream. We shall ask all our friends who believe in equal opportunity, regardless of color, to do the same.*

The manager from the North Omaha location of Reed's responded via the *Omaha Star*, stating, "We don't care if they buy our ice cream or not."

On January 25, 1953, handbills were distributed at the NAACP stating, "AS LONG as a company can refuse to hire Negroes, YOU CAN refuse to buy their products and GET OTHERS to do likewise. Reeds Ice Cream Co. Does Not Hire Negroes....Don't Buy Reeds Ice Cream." North Omaha clubs and churches received handbills as well, and soon, pastors were declaring their support. The Reverend E.T. Streeter urged his congregation at Clair Memorial United Methodist Church to support the project, as did the Reverend Charles Favors at Pilgrim Baptist Church.

The boycott of Reed's Ice Cream North Omaha locations went on through the hot summer months, with volunteers picketing nightly. Efforts impacted profits, and the DePorres Club estimated Reed's loss of business to be as high as 85 percent.

Reed's Ice Cream eventually contracted a black janitor that year, but that was viewed as not enough to show a change in hiring practices. A column in the DePoress Club's newsletter read, "Tell your friends, the Reed's Ice Cream Campaign is still on. A Negro janitor coming in once a day to mop is not Equal Job Opportunities."

Months of picketing and boycotts continued into 1954 before Reed's Ice Cream agreed to change hiring practices. Reed's hired a black saleswoman, Virginia Dixon, in January 1954. To celebrate, the publisher of the *Omaha Star*, Mildred Brown, purchased ice cream from Reed's for members of the DePorres Club.

COMPETITION WITH SUPERMARKETS

In the late 1950s, it became apparent that shopping preferences were starting to shift. Thanks to cheap in-home refrigeration, housewives began to buy ice cream in bulk and keep it at home.

Reed's simply couldn't beat the supermarkets' one-stop shopping convenience. By 1959, Claude Reed had come to the conclusion that they had to get into the wholesale business or add in sandwiches. In the end, they simply closed.

The ice cream stands disappeared eventually. The company's manufacturing plant on North Twenty-Fourth Street continued on under different ownership. Reed turned his attention to his other businesses, Whirla-Whip and Chubbyville.

Chapter 9

TRENTINO'S AND ANGIE'S

Feeding Little Italy for Eight Decades with Steakhouse after Steakhouse on Tenth Street

The long-running Italian restaurant Trentino's resided in the heart of Omaha's Little Italy. It started in 1933 as a small hamburger joint at 1112 South Tenth Street and grew to a traditional Italian steakhouse known for choice meat and spaghetti.

Trentino's was co-owned and operated by Sam Firmature and his wife, Helen; her sister, Louise, and her husband, Anthony "Tony" Salerno. The Firmatures and the Salernos are families that have been fixtures in the Omaha restaurant scene through the years. It was a family-run business, through and through. One of Louise's great-granddaughters, Kim, recalled working there as a girl folding napkins and preparing food.

Prices in Little Italy were lower than other areas in Omaha, particularly on the western edge of the city. In 1939, you could get a U.S. choice steak, spaghetti, French fries, salad and a drink for $0.50 at Trentino's. As an Italian steakhouse, there were a lot of meat options on the menu, from T-bone and roast prime rib to center-cut pork chops. In the 1950s, a T-bone was $3.95, with the same sides as before. Italian dinners included tufoli imbottite, a dish consisting of large macaroni shells stuffed with chopped sirloin and then baked in a casserole, for $1.75. Trentino's homemade ground sirloin–stuffed ravioli was $1.50.

Trentino's also served a variety of pizzas, which in the 1950s cost between $0.95 and $2.50, as well as sandwiches and seafood entrées. One of the restaurant's specialties was tournedos of beef tenderloin in Madeira sauce with mushrooms, vegetables and "assorted tidbits" for $3.25. The tenderloin

Trentino's exterior. Trentino's was in Little Italy from 1933 to 1976. *Courtesy Larry Richling.*

of beef en brochette served on wild rice and topped with mushroom sauce was another specialty entrée. For a couple on a date, they could order Trentino's Italian Dinner for Two, which for $6.00 came with breaded veal parmesan, tufoli and Italian sausage with mostaccioli, minestrone soup, antipasto, salad, beverages and choice of spumoni or cannoli.

Tony Salerno passed away in 1962, and soon after, Louise left Trentino's to reopen Italian Gardens, which was not too far away from the restaurant. Sam Firmature took full ownership of Trentino's after that.

The restaurant closed for a short stint due to a fire in 1968. The fire reportedly caused about $250,000 worth of damage. Columnist Peter Citron in the *Omaha World-Herald* wrote that Trentino's reopened the following year and was "remodeled handsomely."

Angie's Opens

The Firmature family had been operating Trentino's for about forty years before Sam Firmature decided it was time to retire. Trentino's closed in 1976. Shortly thereafter, Jim "Barney" Bonofede purchased the building, saying it was a shame to let it sit empty.

Barney Bonofede opened Angie's in 1977, which was named after his sister, Angie Bonofede. The restaurant's full name was Angie's Restaurant and Cocktail Lounge, but just calling it Angie's is what stuck.

The look of the restaurant was totally changed, and it became a typical steakhouse. The new look was designed by Charlie Stark, who redesigned interiors for Omaha locales like the nightclub The 20s and the restaurant Salvatore's, owned by Barney's brother. The interior was dark, with red being the prevailing color of the décor. The tables were covered with white tablecloths. The walls had etched mirrors, and arches divided the dining room. Bronze-like statues were mounted on panels. The only thing Stark kept in his redesign from the Trentino's days were the chandeliers.

One year later, Citron, the *Omaha World-Herald* columnist, cited it among other new restaurants helping with the rebirth of the neighborhood.

Another columnist for the *Omaha World-Herald*—a sportswriter—wrote that Angie's had three things going for it: the "Nebraska Sports Hall of Fame Room, with its extensive photo gallery; chef Lou Turco's pepper steaks, hailed as Omaha's finest since the days of the Colony Club; and the banana cream pie."

Fred Vacanti, Angie Bonofede's son, recalled many things about the restaurant, from the sports room to the spaghetti sauce. The sauce was his favorite. Angie used her mother's recipe to make it. She and her husband would prepare large batches of the sauce for the restaurant, as well as some of the specialties on the menu.

ANGIE'S AND THE UNDERWORLD

Angie's did a lot for the neighborhood, but there was a darker side to the restaurant. From the beginning, as chronicled in *Cigars and Wires: The Omaha Underworld's Early Years*, Barney Bonofede had ties with key figures of the Kansas City underworld, often entertaining them at his restaurant during the Ak-Sar-Ben racing season.

He also hired a bar manager, Coonie Dinovitz, who had ties to the Kansas City Syndicate, and one of his regulars in 1981 was Patrick O'Brien, another figure in the Kansas City mafia. It was no surprise, then, that the Omaha Police Department monitored the restaurant.

The gambling that took place at Angie's eventually led an indictment of Barney Bonofede and ten others for conducting an illegal gambling business. Bonofede and four others pleaded guilty to the charge; the others pleaded no contest. The five who pleaded guilty were sent to federal prison.

The author of *Cigars and Wires* charged that these indictments and convictions proved deals were made between Omaha's underworld and the more organized Kansas City underworld.

AFTER ANGIE'S

Angie's Restaurant remained in business for twenty-five years following Bonofede's conviction. Angie's was one of the go-to lunch spots for downtown employees in the 1980s and 1990s. In 1991, it was named favorite business lunch by readers in an *Omaha World-Herald* Toast of the Town survey.

A decade later, business had dwindled. The location was a challenge for its owners, and the anticipated resurgence of the Old Market had not quite begun. Construction on the nearby Tenth Street Bridge affected business, as well. On top of that, customers were aging, and there was stiff competition with restaurants trying to attract the new generation of restaurant-goers.

Angie's eventually closed in February 2007.

Five months later, with much of the same look as Angie's—and the same chandeliers as Trentino's—Lucky's Ten-O-One Restaurant and Lounge opened in its place. Owners John and Mary Jo Begley updated a few things—paint, carpet and wall coverings—plus they added a 1973 Wurlitzer jukebox and Omaha memorabilia, particularly that of other Omaha restaurants and steakhouses.

Lucky's was open for just a year, closing in June 2008.

Nancy Mammel purchased the land that the restaurant sat on and donated it to Blue Barn Theatre. The troupe built its new home there, as well as space for other tenants. The first show performed at Blue Barn Theatre was *The Grown Up*, which opened on September 24, 2015.

Even with a thriving theater scene, there are some who still think back to the steakhouse days. Vacanti said, even nine years after Angie's closed, he hears from people who miss it. He hears from people who ate lunch there nearly every day, and they tell him they sure do wish it was back open. "You get used to something, and then when it's gone, you really miss it."

Chapter 10

PICCOLO PETE'S

The Story of How a Piccolo and a Caniglia Created a Beloved City Icon

Piccolo Pete's Restaurant was one of Omaha's longest-running Italian steakhouses, among the best and most beloved there ever was. Its beginning was a small one that didn't hint at what it would become. The restaurant became an Omaha icon, frequented by average citizens and Omaha's most famous billionaire, Warren Buffett. Many residents mourned when the restaurant's eighty-one-year run ended.

The building at 2202 South Twentieth Street was once a blacksmith shop and a saloon before Sicilian immigrant Joseph Piccolo purchased it and opened a grocery store in 1922. In 1933, one of his sons, Anthony Piccolo, was in charge when he turned it into a beer garden, and Piccolo Pete's Restaurant was born.

The name Piccolo Pete was inspired by a popular song about a piccolo player named, as one might have guessed, Pete. There were no actual "Petes" in the Piccolo family, though a few boys in the family picked up the nickname "Piccolo Pete."

Anthony had just married Grace Caniglia when he opened the establishment, on November 25, 1933, making it the oldest of the Caniglia family dynasty's restaurants. Caniglia's signature steakhouse didn't open until 1946, and Grace's five brothers—Ross, Lou, Eli, Yano and Al—didn't open their own popular Omaha restaurants until even later.

Prohibition ended the same year the restaurant opened. The scene at Piccolo's on the first night alcohol was legal could have been straight out of a movie: customers spilled out into the street, toasting with mugs of beer all the way down the block.

Piccolo's dining room. *Courtesy Tim Trudell.*

The bar at Piccolo Pete's. *Courtesy the Durham Museum Photo Archive.*

Piccolo's advertised itself as Omaha's newest and most beautiful beer garden, with the atmosphere and dance floor that everyone's heart desired. Young couples danced under the crystal ball hanging over the terrazzo floors.

In those days, the restaurant was in the heart of South Omaha's hustle and bustle. That part of town was multi-ethnic. "The neighborhood was a melting pot: Polish, Italian, Bohemian," said Donna Sheehan. Sheehan was one of Anthony Piccolo's daughters, and in 2013, she described the early days of the restaurant to a reporter with *Saveur* magazine: it was a madhouse each night until 1:00 a.m.

Food was added to the menu soon after, and Piccolo's became more like a traditional restaurant. The menu was heavy on steaks and chops. In the early days, New York cuts were $2.75. Many dinners were less than $2.00, including barbecue pork ribs for $1.75 and breaded veal cutlet for $1.35. The restaurant did serve seafood, ranging in price from $1.35 to $3.75. Italian specialties were spaghetti and meat sauce or with meatballs, mostaccioli and ravioli. Two types of pizza were available, hamburger or cheese, for $1.00 and $0.85, respectively. The children's menu had regular dinner entrées at children's portions.

The crystal ball over Piccolo's dance floor. *Courtesy Tim Trudell.*

Two men dining at Piccolo Pete's in 1975. *Courtesy the Durham Museum Photo Archive.*

Half the menu was the wine, beer and liquor list. The menu helpfully paired food with the wine: the reds were "most complimentary to red meats and cheese"; the whites "blend particularly well with shellfish and lighter meats"; and the rose wine, Alamaden Grenach Rose at $2.50 a bottle, was the "ONE wine that goes with everything." Items were subject to tax when dancing occurred.

Eventually, tables covered the dance floor, and the era of dancing under the crystal ball was replaced with the days of dining under it. The restaurant expanded its dining area over the years. In 1985, the seating grew from 240 people to 310. Still, on the weekends, customers could expect a thirty-minute or longer wait to get seated.

Piccolo's was a family-oriented restaurant with Italian dishes that were low priced. In the tradition of Italian steakhouses in Omaha, pasta was the side dish of choice. In the case of Piccolo's, it was mostaccioli with a scoop of red sauce in the middle of the heap. Another popular side was hash browns, described with mouth-watering detail by a *Saveur* magazine reporter in 2013: "shredded potatoes fried in butter in a small steel pan until they fuse into a golden disk with a crunchy exterior encasing a creamy, fluffy center."

Above: Dinnertime at Piccolo's. *Courtesy Tim Trudell.*

Left: The entrance to Piccolo Pete's with the iconic neon sign of a piccolo player. *Courtesy David Vonk.*

In the 1980s, most dinners were under $6.00, save for a few steak entrées. A few of the choices in 1985 included pork chops and roast sirloin of beef with brown sauce, each costing $5.95. The most expensive item was the chateaubriand, which served two people for $21.95, followed by the seafarer's choice featuring broiled small lobster tail and a filet for $13.75.

Prime rib was one of the memorable beef dishes, simply seasoned with a mix of garlic, dried basil, dried oregano, celery salt and a lot of black pepper. It was served with Rotella's Italian bread.

PICCOLO'S NUMBER ONE SUPPORTER

Warren Buffett poses with a student from Ohio State University's Fisher College of Business at Piccolo Pete's. Buffett regularly took groups of students to dine at Piccolo's. *Courtesy Aaron Friedman.*

One of the restaurant's biggest fans was billionaire Warren Buffett, whose patronage helped keep the restaurant afloat in its seventh and eighth decades of business. In 2007, a CNBC feature on him included a stop at Piccolo Pete's. During *Warren Buffett: The Billionaire Next Door—Going Global*, Buffett talked about his appreciation for the restaurant: "I love the food. The two sisters are just terrific that run it, ah, but it just couldn't be a better place. So I take, if A-Rod's in town, Jeff Immelt [General Electric chairman and CEO] is coming into town tomorrow, we'll have dinner there, whomever, and they always like it and we always finish with a root beer float." Buffett got a big root beer float every visit, and his dining guests usually did too.

So loyal was Buffett that he would bring shareholders, business partners, hundreds of business students, Major League Baseball players and anyone else visiting in Omaha. A few of his guests have included actor-economist Ben Stein, Microsoft co-founder Bill Gates and IBM CEO Virginia Rometty.

Buffett told the *Omaha World-Herald* in 2014, "I consider Piccolo's like a neighborhood tavern, an easy place to kick back and talk about whatever you want to talk about. The people are friendly, the food is great, the prices are good. They'll have me as a customer the rest of my life."

PICCOLO'S EIGHTY-ONE-YEAR RUN ENDS

The owners during the restaurant's final days were two of Anthony Piccolo's daughters, Donna Sheehan and Dee Graves. They decided the final night of the restaurant should be a bittersweet New Year's Eve party in 2015. Sheehan told the *Omaha World-Herald*, "We said that we came in with music and we're going out with music. We want to do something special for our staff. They stuck it out with us since we announced the closing. They've gone way above and beyond anything we've asked of them."

On the last day, regulars came to remember the restaurant fondly. Sixty-eight-year-old Sandy Bogema had been going to the restaurant since she was three. As she ate her favorite meal, a T-bone steak, she told the *Omaha World-Herald*, "We've had so many celebrations here that I can't count. I remember we used to come every Saturday night after church."

A part of Piccolo Pete's lives on in the form of a food truck. Sheehan's son Scott Anthony Sheehan started Anthony Piccolo's Mobile Venue, and it can still be found on the streets of Omaha.

Chapter 11

ITALIAN GARDENS

A Bomb Couldn't Stop Italian Gardens from Opening and Succeeding

In 1932, Prohibition was lifted across the country.

Except in Nebraska.

The conservative state remained dry a full year later.

Except in Omaha.

While the rest of the state wanted a ban on the vice, the residents of the river city wanted cheap alcohol readily available. Prohibition in Omaha had the same effect as it did elsewhere in the country: it created more crime while people continued to drink.

Bombings and murder were tied to racketeering feuds. The violence almost caused the end of one of Omaha's longest-running restaurants, Italian Gardens, before it had a chance to open.

*****

Italian Gardens was not a welcomed addition to the Little Italy neighborhood in Omaha. When a former bootlegger, Giuseppina Marcuzzo, decided in 1934 to open the restaurant at 1228 South Sixth Street for her son Mondo, her friends warned her. They meant well. They asked her if the venture could possibly be successful.

But there was something simmering in the neighborhood that they surely had noticed. About four dozen people in the neighborhood had signed petitions against the restaurant opening. One man who signed the petition, Sam Letta, said he signed "to keep the neighborhood clean."

Giuseppina Marcuzzo, *second from left*, in front of Italian Gardens. *Courtesy Louie Marcuzzo.*

One woman said she'd heard a man ominously say it would never open, even though it was days from doing so.

Giuseppina Marcuzzo's friends had a good reason to be concerned. For two years, the city had been terrorized by bombings. There'd been ten since 1932. And the recent murder of liquor racketeer Clarence Hanfelt was still fresh on everyone's minds.

But the date was set. Giuseppina and Mondo Marcuzzo were determined to open Italian Gardens on October 11, 1934. The $10,000 investment would have a terrazza dance floor. A bar. Elaborate fixtures throughout.

On the morning of October 10, a bomb exploded inside the restaurant. The 4:30 a.m. blast shattered windows in nearby homes. The sound was so loud that most around Omaha heard it. The police commissioner heard the bomb from his residence near Forty-Eighth and Fort Streets—nearly five miles away—and rushed to the scene, along with other police officers.

Giuseppina Marcuzzo was reported to have run to the scene, as well, but fainted as she approached. Mondo and his sister, Josephine, carried her home. The site was grim. Bricks littered the entrance. The rear bar was blown over.

After the bombing, police questioned the petition signers. There was some speculation that Hanfelt's murder was connected to the bombing. An opinion piece in the *Omaha World-Herald* the next day suggested the bombings and murder were due to the ongoing racketeer feud and "underworld defiance." Days earlier, Mondo's brother Angelo had contributed money for a flower arrangement sent to Hanfelt's funeral.

No one was charged for the bombing. Speculation remains on whether the building was bombed by the petitioners or from the result of a feud.

ITALIAN GARDENS CHANGES IN OWNERSHIP

Giuseppina Marcuzzo did open Italian Gardens, making it a full-fledged restaurant. Her son Mondo went on to own a bar elsewhere in Omaha.

The first few years of the restaurant were successful enough to allow renovations. In 1937, Giuseppina remodeled and redecorated Italian Gardens. That summer, air conditioning was a new feature they used to lure customers. The booths were now covered in leather. Marketed as Omaha's newest cocktail bar and grill, on December 2, they celebrated with a reopening weekend and gave each female diner a rose.

Dinner specialties at the time were spaghetti, ravioli, fried chicken, T-bone steaks and Italian sausage. All meals were served with soup, salad, potatoes and dessert, plus a choice of coffee or wine for fifty to seventy-five cents.

Italian Gardens also touted itself as a mixed drinks specialist, serving Old Granddad and Old Taylor whiskeys.

Giuseppina Marcuzzo eventually passed the restaurant to two other sons. Business was so good that the Marcuzzos ran Italian Gardens until the 1960s. They sold the restaurant to Salvatore "Sonny" Nocita. It became known as Sonny's Italian Gardens and Cocktail Lounge.

Joe Marcuzzo, son of Giuseppina Marcuzzo, tending bar at Italian Gardens. *Courtesy Louie Marcuzzo.*

The Italian Gardens baseball team in front of the restaurant. *Courtesy Lou Marcuzzo.*

Above: Dinner at Italian Gardens in the 1930s. *Courtesy Louie Marcuzzo.*

Right: Members of the Brandeis family in front of Italian Gardens. The first location of Brandeis, the popular chain of department stores, was started by Jonas Brandeis in Omaha. *Courtesy Louie Marcuzzo.*

It remained under the helm of Nocita for only a short while. He passed away at age forty-four on March 30, 1961. Louise Salerno took over operation of Italian Gardens in 1962. She co-owned the downtown Italian fixture Trentino's from 1933 for nearly three decades before running Italian Gardens. She left Trentino's after her husband, Tony, passed away.

TWO SIDES TO LOUISE SALERNO

Salerno is a complex figure in Omaha's restaurant history. She is remembered as a motherly figure by many and eventually was honored for her charitable work, but her early years in Omaha were not without scandal.

Born in Carlentini, Sicily, she came to the United States when she was eight. She eventually married Tony Salerno. Some described Tony and his brother Sebastiano, or "Yano," as padrones, assisting new immigrants in Omaha, helping them find apartments and set up banking services.

The brothers, however, were also reputably bootleggers. Tony and Yano had run-ins with the law for assault and intimidation. On December 13, 1930, Louise and Tony's home was raided, but no liquor was found. Eleven months later, another raid yielded twenty-five gallons of liquor. Louise and her husband were arrested in their home on November 28, 1932, for threatening a witness not to testify against them for the Bureau of Prohibition.

Louise Salerno put those days behind her when she and Tony became co-owners of Trentino's the following year. Thirty years later, she was running her own restaurant.

The food of Italian Gardens under Salerno's direction was Sicilian. Her recipes were not written down, at least not at first. She'd prepare food the way her mother did, without a measuring spoon.

In a column for *Food & Spirit*, writer Bill MacKenzie recalled dining in Salerno's Italian Gardens. He wrote that he felt like family there and remained on a first-name basis with Salerno and her daughter, Sara:

> *The place was tiny...but on a couple of occasions when our extended family came to town they would close the restaurant to the public and it became all ours. Once, when my mom had surgery and was off her feet for a week, word somehow got out to the Salerno ladies, and one evening a car pulled up to our house, and several large trays of salad, spaghetti and meatballs, lasagna and yes, toasted raviolis were delivered to our front door...gratis. Now that's Amore.*

Salerno ran Italian Gardens for about seven years before closing it down in 1969. Nearly a decade later, she explained to the *Omaha World-Herald* the reason behind closing it: she got tired of prima donna chefs.

Later in life, Salerno made amends for her past. For her service over the years, she received an outstanding service award from Southeast Civic Center in 1976 and a humanitarian award from the Creighton University alumni association in 1979. University officials called her a "mother-type figure" to those who worked and studied at the old St. Catherine and St. Joseph hospitals.

Eventually, Salerno did write down her recipes, sharing her culinary knowledge through the cookbook *Buon Appetito*, which she wrote with her daughter. To create the book, Salerno would prepare a dish with her daughter by her side, weighing each ingredient. *Buon Appetito* was published in 1976 and went into reprint in the succeeding years. It included Salerno-style recipes for lasagna, fettucine, chicken Sicilian and cannoli.

Le Café de Paris Opens

The sign in the parking lot of Le Café de Paris. *Courtesy Kevin Reiner.*

The restaurant Le Café de Paris opened at the end of 1969. It was a rare five-star restaurant in the Midwest. It didn't exactly have a great start. By 1971, the restaurant was struggling. Peter Citron, an *Omaha World-Herald* columnist, wrote that some people found the small restaurant "too much for them in price and attention." Even so, the restaurant catered to an elite crowd that kept it in business for decades.

Under the direction of owner Ivan Konsul, dinner was described as a culinary adventure, lasting two to three hours. It had a reputation for being one of the few restaurants in Omaha where wine service was properly done.

The menu had no prices and French names, with small descriptions in English for some. Diners could begin a meal with hors d'oeuvres like Iranian caviar, escargot, fresh mussels or white asparagus. Some of the house specialties included grilled lobster, baby pheasant flambéed tableside, Indian lamb curry served with mongoose and filet mignon Monte Carlo. For dessert, the options included an apple tart, caramel custard and two types of crepes flambéed tableside.

The restaurant was highly regarded, not just in Nebraska, but throughout the country. For decades, it earned awards and landed on lists. *Holiday-Travel* magazine noted it in 1979 for its dining award. In 1982, it was described as "A Hidden Jewel in the Midwest" in a *Fortune* magazine story. When the Distinguished Restaurants of North America honor began in 1993, Le Café de Paris was honored in it annually.

After nearly forty years, Le Café de Paris closed following the death of the owner's wife.

After Le Café de Paris

John and Allison Querry opened Q Consumables in the space on September 27, 2010. The menu was seasonally based and made from scratch, with entrées served simply and without garnish. The price point was more palatable than Le Café de Paris for the average diner.

The Querrys maintained an easygoing atmosphere, with trendy indie music playing on the speakers. They removed the restaurant's carpeting to discover a green and red terrazzo floor that added even more character to the eclectically decorated room.

A little more than a year after Q Consumables opened, John Querry collapsed and passed away.

Jeff Camp, the former owner of Trovato's and a former executive chef at French Café, opened a second incarnation of Italian Gardens in December 2012. It was a quick turnaround. Camp recalled taking only six weeks to open his restaurant, and that included getting permits and inspections, including receiving the fire permit the day before opening.

The food at Italian Gardens was meant to be a mix of small plates of regional Italian cuisine and heaping plates of pasta, an expectation for any Italian restaurant that opened in Omaha. Some dishes were nostalgic, with the kitchen using recipes from Louise Salerno and Rena Trovato, the original co-owner of Trovato's, including her veal Parmesan and sweet marinara.

Camp opened the restaurant under the assumption that he'd have a lot of support from his neighbors in Little Italy. But the neighborhood crowd never came that first year. The restaurant drew a crowd from West Omaha, and within nine months, Camp realized he'd opened a restaurant in the wrong place.

The second Italian Gardens closed in early 2014. A catering business now operates out of the building.

Chapter 12

ROSE LODGE

Home of Omaha's Favorite Fried Chicken

That chicken.

Ask anyone who was lucky enough to remember dining at Rose Lodge what they remember about the restaurant at Seventy-Eighth and Dodge Streets and they will mention the chicken.

Rose Rose, who ran the restaurant for nearly thirty years before retiring, was proud of her fried chicken recipe. It was something that lived on even after the restaurant shuttered its doors.

Rose was no stranger to the Omaha restaurant scene when Rose Lodge opened up. She had run Rose's at 280 South Sixty-Eighth Avenue before then. When the opening day of Rose Lodge neared, July 3, 1937, it was good business sense to mention chicken in all advertisements for Rose Lodge. It advertised forty-cent fried chicken sandwiches that first month.

People already knew what they were in for.

That chicken.

Rose Lodge opened among farmland, one of its later owners, August Ross, recalled. There was speculation that the old farmhouse Rose Lodge occupied was once a Prohibition-era speakeasy. Word was the garage had a trapdoor leading to a hidden basement room.

Rose Lodge's fried chicken was the big draw. Rose created the "mouth-watering" recipe for the plump, tender, gold-brown chicken. The restaurant also served chicken and noodles, steaks, coleslaw, mashed potatoes with chicken gravy and little bread and butter sandwiches cut into triangles.

Dessert included homemade cream pies, such as banana cream, chocolate cream, graham cracker cream and cocoa cream. They also served cherry pie.

In the Middle of Farmland No More

As big a draw as her chicken was, the restaurant started gaining attention for another reason: location. When Rose was ready to retire in the early 1960s, she found eager buyers. August Ross and his law partner, Bob O'Connor, became owners of Rose Lodge starting in 1965. They knew the land was valuable, as Seventy-Second and Dodge was quickly becoming the center of activity and retail in Omaha.

As it turned out, business kept getting better and better. The reputation for the fried chicken lived on even after Rose's retirement.

The O'Connors continued running Rose Lodge for more than two decades. In 1970, they remodeled the restaurant. The dining room had dark woodwork, and the walls had stuffed animal heads on them. There were additions to the old farmhouse. It now had a large main dining room, one smaller room and a party room. The tables kept a farm look to them, though, with red-and-white checkered tablecloths covering them. Out front, a neon sign for Rose Lodge, complete with a big red rose, let customers know they were at the right place.

But that chicken remained the same, and it continued to bring in crowds.

In the 1970s, a typical night out before an Omaha Knights hockey game would include a stop at Rose Lodge, according to Gary Anderson, author of *Those Were the Knights: The History of Professional Hockey in Omaha*, who mentioned the fried chicken during an interview reflecting on his thirty-year career as University of Nebraska at Omaha's sports information director.

An ad in 1970 stated, "We have had millions of persons enjoy the famous Rose Lodge recipe and these customers are still our best advertisement."

When Land Became Too Valuable

It was business as usual—busy business as usual—for more than a decade under the O'Connor ownership. In an interview with the *Omaha World-Herald* after the purchase was announced in August 31, 1984, O'Connor Jr. said they had sales of about $500,000 a year.

Eventually, the value of the land outgrew even impressive sales like $500,000 a year. O'Connor Jr. and Ross, who were both attorneys, were approached by buyers out of the blue. They didn't know what the buyers' intentions were. But the offer was too good to refuse.

Rose Lodge was sold to Services for Children, Children's Hospital's parent firm, in August 1984. After the purchase, the hospital traded to O'Daniel Olds-Honda for nearby land owned by O'Daniel. O'Daniel built a Honda franchise where Rose Lodge once stood.

One of the cooks at Rose Lodge opened a restaurant in Treynor, Iowa, called the Rose, using the famous recipes. The Rose had memorabilia from Rose Lodge. As many people speculated, it was true—the fried chicken was the same as Rose Rose's beloved recipe.

However, the Rose was eventually closed due to a fire.

Chapter 13

MARCHIO'S ITALIAN CAFÉ

The Steakhouse That Survived World War II Meat Rations

The sign out front of Marchio's Italian Café read "Louis Marchio's Delicious Steaks," but World War II meat rationings almost ended the restaurant. They actually closed the restaurant for some time. However, determined owners weathered the break and returned to run the restaurant for decades to come.

Italian immigrant Louis Marchio began preparing delicious meals out of his home in 1929. Ten years later, he opened Marchio's Italian Café at 4443 South Thirteenth Street on August 15, 1939. The building was white with red trim. Marchio specialized in steaks and chicken dinners in the beginning.

Timing may not have been in Marchio's favor, though. The United States' involvement in World War II affected life on the homefront. Omaha was not exempt from its effects, and to help with the war effort, meat rations were placed on families and restaurants.

Marchio ran into some trouble in 1941 with purchasing more meat rations than he was allotted. In December that year, when restaurants got their first allotment of rations, the owners were asked to provide estimates of the number of patrons they'd have and the total revenue they expected that month. Like other restaurants, Marchio received rations for all patrons during the month, even the ones who just came in for a drink. In all, he got enough for thirty-one thousand meals a month. Under the new regulations, restaurant owners had to keep a daily worksheet and separate food and drink customers. Under those rules, Marchio would only receive 30 percent of the rations as before.

The exterior of Marchio's Italian Café in 1942. *Courtesy the Durham Museum Photo Archive.*

In 1942, the meat ration and a restaurant cap started to hurt business. Some restaurants were resorting to purchasing meat from the black market to stay in business, but not Marchio, who was a World War I veteran. Marchio's was the first restaurant to announce closure for the duration of the meat ration, though Marchio did keep the lounge open. His wife explained that customers had been good to the restaurant but that they'd rather close for the duration of rations than skimp on quality.

The chairman of the South Side ration board told the *Omaha World-Herald* that Marchio's situation was rough, "but under the regulations we were powerless to help him further."

By May 1944, it started to get easier to purchase meats, besides steaks, and a hint of Marchio's reopening was in the air. By the end of November 1944, Marchio's had reopened.

Marchio had another run-in with the law a few years after the ration incident. In March 1946, Marchio's, along with six other restaurants, settled with the government on overcharging for food or mixed drinks. Louis Marchio was ordered to lower the price of T-bone steak from $2.00 to the ceiling price of $1.50. He had to pay the Treasury Department $165.00 for overcharging on steaks. His steakhouse had the most to pay out of the group.

Louis Marchio holding a steak on the day he announced he'd served his last steak until the meat rations would end. *Courtesy the Durham Museum Photo Archive.*

Marchio's became a meeting place for groups such as fraternal orders, as well as sports teams. As popularity grew, Marchio purchased neighboring houses to expand both the restaurant and parking lot.

In 1960, the cost of a T-bone steak rose to $3.50 and the New York cut sirloin was $3.75. All other entrees were less than $3.00, though. Items listed under *I migliori d'Italia* (The Best of Italy) included dishes like veal scaloppini, which was veal served in a white wine sauce with mushrooms. The fried chicken ala Marchio had a special seasoning; the Marchios promised on the menu that "you'll want to become better acquainted with" its flavor.

The Younger Marchio Takes Over

After Louis Marchio passed away, his son, Paul, assumed ownership. Under Paul Marchio's leadership, there was a menu shakeup in 1970. Steaks had been heavily featured on the menu up until then. Paul Marchio decided to add some new Italian dishes into the rotation. Several beef dishes remained, though, including the Marchio Polo specialty, which was sautéed slices of beef tenderloin with spaghetti and mushrooms and tomato sauce. When Louis Marchio invented the dish, filet was a cheap cut of meat. He sold the dish for $0.35 back in the early days, but by 1970, it had gone up to $3.75.

They had a postcard that read, "The distinct flavor of our steaks served with our famous spaghetti has made Marchio's one of the favorite places to dine in Omaha."

New Owners, Same Name

Paul Marchio's health deteriorated in the 1970s. He had two heart attacks. In 1976, Arlan Broomes and Frank Bianco purchased Marchio's Italian Café.

Broomes and Bianco both retired from the U.S. Air Force to manage the restaurant. Broomes and his wife were fairly new residents of the city at the time, but they quickly understood that the restaurant was an institution in the area. They did not change the name and kept many of the recipes. Paul's son, Paul Marchio II, stayed on as a cook.

There was a three-alarm fire in the restaurant in 1980. Though the building wasn't destroyed, it was heavily damaged. The restaurant had to undergo considerable remodeling. The Broomeses added archways where walls once were and whitened the interior with stucco. It looked more like the Colosseum than it once had.

Marchio's closed after forty-six years in operation in 1985.

In July 1990, the South Omaha staple Howard's Charro relocated to the building and remains in business today.

Chapter 14

HILLTOP HOUSE

The Restaurant on the Hill That Balanced Elegance and Comfort Food

Traces of one of Omaha's most beloved restaurants that inspired newspaper columns from the River City to the Windy City can still be seen in Omaha. The sign at Forty-Ninth and Dodge Streets reads "Hilltop House," but what was once a popular place for upscale dining is now offices and apartments.

Hilltop House had humble beginnings but quickly grew in popularity, surviving through the meat ration days of World War II and inflation in the 1970s.

*****

Raymond and Mildred Matson opened Hilltop House as a single dining room with a fireplace on January 28, 1941. The location on Dodge Street was in fact near a hilltop, just a smidge away from the precise top to allow for a parking lot. The property was owned by Mildred and her mother.

The Colonial-style décor with antiques throughout created its homey feel. One longtime customer said the restaurant resembled an English tearoom. The food only added to the coziness. The restaurant served comfort food, and it served it up well. Among the home-cooked entrées were generous portions of baked chicken and pork patties. Specialties were creamed chicken on hot tea biscuits, chicken salad and cinnamon rolls. The dessert options were immense.

The Matsons started Hilltop House on a small budget. Rumor has it that they borrowed money to make change on their opening night. But those meager early days did not last long. The restaurant's popularity grew and, with it, the restaurant's space.

Hilltop House Expansion

In the restaurant's early days, the Matsons had to contend with World War II and its effect on the homefront. Omaha had to institute meat rationing for the general population and restaurants in 1941. It hurt a lot of businesses before it ended in 1944, and Hilltop House could not escape the effects. The Matsons had to stop serving lunches so that there was enough meat for dinner guests.

Hilltop House persevered, and after the war, the restaurant began to outgrow its dining room. Its growth was tremendous. The restaurant expanded two times within its first ten years. It started out with seventy-five-person seating in the Pine Room, which later was renamed the Harbor Room. In 1947, it added the Garden Room, with a capacity for thirty people. Then, in 1951, it expanded by joining the restaurant with its neighbor, the Mildred Apartments, which resulted in the addition of Cape Cod Room, Danish Room, Duck Room, the Red Rooster bar and lounge and the tiled corridor.

The Red Rooster was a natural extension of the home-like feeling in the main restaurant. It felt like you were being entertained in someone's home. Continuing the Colonial style, there was overstuffed furniture, captain's chairs and a fireplace surrounded by walls of knotty pine, exposed wood beams and a chestnut ceiling. The drink of choice in the bar was called the Gold Cadillac.

For years to come, Hilltop House was the preferred meeting place for many and a destination for tourists in the know. Private events were regularly held there, from club meetings to senior citizen backgammon tournaments, prenuptials and book clubs.

It was a family-friendly restaurant with a kids' menu. In fact, *Chicago Tribune* writer Stevenson Swanson grew up in Omaha and recalled spending every Thanksgiving of his childhood at Hilltop House—except for one year. In a 1982 column for the *Tribune*, Swanson remembered how his mother won a turkey when he was eleven years old and decided to prepare a feast for the family. Swanson anticipated a great meal but was surprised and ultimately disappointed—he wanted a hamburger from Hilltop House.

THE BEST DAYS AT HILLTOP HOUSE

Hubert "Hub" Piechota was hired at Hilltop House in 1946, working as both a manager and chef for decades. His wife, Rosemarie, worked with him as a hostess from 1962 to 1981. The restaurant's best years were largely thanks to Piechota and his elegantly prepared meals. He received awards throughout his career, including back-to-back Restaurateur of the Year in Nebraska awards in 1979 and 1980. In 1995, he was inducted into the Omaha Hospitality Hall of Fame. Ray Matson was inducted the year before.

The house specialty during Piechota's time at the restaurant was the roast prime rib, which in 1974 cost $5.75. Other regular items on the menu were quintessential comfort foods, including boneless pork loin served with wild rice and brown gravy for $4.45 and chicken fried steak with country gravy for $4.25. Hot homemade rolls accompanied meals.

Hints of a troubled restaurant popped up even during Piechota's high points. Rumors swirled in 1974 that the restaurant had been sold; it had not. A few years later, there were some indications of a financial strain on the restaurant. In October 1978, Piechota told the *Omaha World-Herald* about cost-cutting measures at the restaurant spurred by inflation. Some of the measures included staggering hours and not replacing employees who quit. To reduce energy expenses, Piechota said staff would turn off power and air conditioning when not needed and leave the ovens and gas ranges off until it was time to prepare meals. They even switched from cloth napkins to paper during lunch and quit putting ice in water glasses.

In 1979, more rumors circulated. There was one about the restaurant being turned into a retirement home. Another, even worse, was that it would turn into a fast-food joint. Piechota retired that year following a disabling heart attack.

In July 1979, the rumors were put to rest. The Matsons were going to retire after nearly thirty-nine years at Hilltop House on December 25, 1979, and the restaurant was going to have new owners. The story goes that the Matsons were flying back from London on the same plane as Dr. Wally Duff. By the time they'd landed, Duff was contemplating buying the restaurant. After conferring with other potential co-owners, Duff bought the restaurant with attorneys Jim Schumacher and Dave Karnes. The trio told the Hilltop House employees that they had no intention of major changes. Duff and Karnes eventually stepped aside, and Schumacher and Marcia Baer became sole co-owners.

The new owners were determined to revamp the Red Rooster bar in order to draw in a "young, sophisticated" crowd. The loud music was going away, and they planned on catering to diet-conscious clientele.

The restaurant didn't fare well under new ownership and a new chef. Soon, dinner service was limited to a few nights a week and then eventually down to one. The last meal was served on June 6, 1981.

AFTER HILLTOP HOUSE

After Hilltop's closure, an announcement followed that shocked some clientele: the restaurant would become a Mexican eatery. Bob and Katie Mackie opened a second Roberto's location at Hilltop House's location on August 11, 1981. Roberto's served Mexican food but also had a large American menu. The Red Rooster was renamed Margarita-ville.

Jeff Jordan wrote in the *Omaha World-Herald* on August 21, 1981, that he thought the "clientele who so loyally supported the Midtown landmark over the years would not be disappointed" by the new restaurant. Even with $500,000 in renovations, the interior would look familiar. Colonial touches had been replaced by "tasteful displays of greenery, dried floral arrangements, copperware, and occasional mirror or painting," but those changes you'd have to really look for, according to Jordan.

Hilltop regulars did return to dine there. There are stories of some of the few regulars who did return trying to move tables in order to be at "their" tables.

Roberto's and its Margarita-ville bar did not last in that location. The building was converted to apartments and offices in 1985.

Chapter 15

THE ORIGINAL CANIGLIA'S PIZZARIA AND STEAKHOUSE

They Brought Pizza to Omaha and Raised a Family of Restaurateurs

The Caniglia family's restaurant empire in Omaha all began with a burnt pizza pie in 1946.

From that, the Original Caniglia's Pizzaria and Steakhouse was born—a restaurant that would introduce pizza to Omaha and set the standard for Italian steakhouses in the city. At one point, there were eight restaurants connected to the Caniglia family in some way.

"The Caniglia family deserves a lot of credit for its success—and also for its role in laying the groundwork for the vibrant restaurant scene that Omahans enjoy today," explained an *Omaha World-Herald* editorial in 2005.

*****

Cirno Caniglia had run a bakery at 1114 South Seventh Street for more than twenty years when his family conceived an idea to open a restaurant. The Caniglia bakery's neighborhood, Little Italy, was a thriving community of well-supported Italian-operated establishments. In 1940, there were fourteen Italian specialty restaurants and steakhouses, forty Italian chefs and one hundred bars and taverns with two hundred Italian bartenders. The bakery was a stone's throw from Orsi bakery, and slightly farther afield, there was Rotella's.

Little Italy was more than businesses, though. It had a convivial atmosphere. A publication by the Works Progress Administration described a scene in 1941:

A photo of the Caniglia men—Yano, Ross, Lou, Dad, Al and Eli—appeared on restaurant menus above the words "Caniglias Welcome You to The pizzeria." *Courtesy Metropolitan Community College Institute for the Culinary Arts.*

> *The streets of Little Italy resound with the noise and laughter of many children. The stores display foods found dear to the heart of the people—salamis, cheeses, olive oil, macaroni, spaghetti, braided lengths of garlic and strings of gleaming red peppers drying in the sun. In season, the Italians make pasta pomo d'oro, a highly seasoned tomato sauce, and the appetite-teasing odor of it pervades the entire neighborhood.*

Eli Caniglia, Cirno and Giovanna's third-eldest son, was the one who first tried pizza. Eli was in Baltimore in 1945 awaiting military orders to fly to England when he encountered something similar to *cucurene*, a double-crusted meat and cheese pastry his mom used to make. Her *cucurene* was nothing special, but the pizza Eli had was something different. He wrote home to his dad, Cirno, saying they "could make a fortune with something called pizza."

He returned home and convinced his family they should introduce Omaha to pizza. On August 3, 1946, the pizzeria opened and served its first slice of commercially made pizza. Eli's brother Yano was the one to burn the first attempt, but things worked themselves out after that.

Caniglia's Pizzaria and Steakhouse was born.

Home of Pizza and Steaks

"Caniglias Welcome You to the Pizzaria" read the menu, right below a picture labeled "Yano, Ross, Lou, Dad, Al and Eli." Pizza was the big draw to Caniglias at first—though non-Italians had to be taught how to eat it. A family could get a cheese and tomato pizza for fifty-nine cents in 1954; a double-crust hamburger pizza was just thirty cents more. The Caniglia's Super Special Pizza at the restaurant was topped with tomato, cheese, anchovies, salami, pepperoni, sausage and onions.

The *Omaha World-Herald* wrote, "From the year of creation into the 1960s, Caniglia's was almost a shrine for a ballooning population of aficionados of pizza, as well as the steaks and the other Italian items that were quickly added to the menu."

What began with pizza grew to something much bigger thanks to steaks and a philosophy on service: give customers hearty servings and good hospitality. It would set the benchmark for all Italian steakhouses to follow.

The steaks were reasonably priced and served with a lot of food. One could order a small sirloin for $2.50 in 1965, or dine on a Tuesday and Wednesday, when it was priced at $1.75. The menu also included fried spring chicken, homemade Italian sausage, breaded veal cutlets and a few seafood dishes, including fried fresh channel catfish, African lobster tail drawn in butter and fried frog legs with tartar sauce. The only dessert available in the early days was spumoni, if you had room for it.

Cirno and Giovanna's son Ross took over the restaurant in the 1970s, and then grandsons Bob, Chuck and Ross Caniglia took over and ran the restaurant for the next thirty years. The trio were no strangers to the restaurant, having worked there since they were children. "I used to get a dime every time I ran a takeout order back to the kitchen," Chuck told the *Omaha World-Herald*.

The restaurant was so popular that it expanded three times. By 1984, it could seat 210 people in its four dining rooms, including one just for non-smokers.

By 1984, the pizza was mainly a takeout order, with steak and Italian specialties being the featured menu items in the evenings. The portions were still huge. Petite prime rib was $6.09 or $8.19 for a regular cut. A fifteen-ounce T-bone was $7.49 on Wednesday nights. With the veal Parmesan, the veal filled the entire plate.

An End of an Era

The Original Caniglia's Pizzaria and Steakhouse—the "original" part added decades after the family's successful ventures in launching other restaurants—could not be sustained forever. The owners placed some blame on the casinos for Caniglia's dwindling business. Bob Caniglia told the *Omaha World-Herald* that he remembered the day Bluffs Run Greyhound Park opened a slot-machine casino: "It was just like a neutron bomb went off in here. The building's standing. All the people are gone."

His brother Chuck said of it, "We thought we could outlast them when they first opened. We've been through a lot of stuff—recessions, wars. But nothing is like a casino."

There was an additional concern for Bob, Chuck and Ross. Given the state of business, the older guys didn't think it would have been right to hand it down to the fourth generation.

On August 7, 2005, the Original Caniglia's Pizzaria and Steakhouse served its last meal. It was nearly sixty-nine years to the day after the first pizza was served there. On the restaurant's last day, brothers Al and Yano were there. They told the *Omaha World-Herald* they never expected the restaurant to close in their lifetime.

Chapter 16

FAIR DEAL CAFÉ

The Diner Known as Omaha's Black City Hall and Home to the Best Soul Food in Town

The 1950s were the golden age for North Omaha. The neighborhood had a thriving jazz scene that attracted some of the best touring bands to Omaha. North Twenty-Fourth Street was the hub of activity. If any business was going to open in North Omaha, North Twenty-Fourth Street was the obvious location. In those days, most businesses were owned by Jewish or Italian men who were mostly white immigrants to the city. But not Fair Deal Café. Its owner, Charlie Hall, was black. It was rare for a black man to run a restaurant in Omaha in that era.

For decades to come, Fair Deal Café would be one of the few constants in a tumultuous and changing neighborhood.

*****

Fair Deal Café's early days are not well documented. Some say it opened in the 1940s. For certain, the restaurant was up and running at 2118 North Twenty-Fourth Street by 1950.

Charlie Hall started working at Fair Deal Café around 1953 after spending some time working as a butcher. Six months after he began working at the restaurant, the owners moved away and left the place to him.

Hall met his second wife, Audentria (better known as Dennie), at Fair Deal Café. They worked together for four decades: she serving breakfast and he serving dinner. "We worked together over 40 years and we never argued. We were partners and friends and mates and lovers," Charlie told *The Reader*.

The food the Halls served was soul food, and many would say it was the best soul food in the city. Charlie served up everything from greens and black-eyed peas to chitterlings and neck bones. Breakfast fixings included grits and potatoes.

Charlie managed to keep prices low by shopping sales and working closely with the butcher to get the best cut of meats at the lowest price. Thanks to his savvy shopping and culinary skills, he kept prices low and the food good. In 1957, customers could get a Mother's Day all-you-can-eat chicken dinner for just $1.50.

In those early days, the restaurant was so busy that the Halls would open at 5:00 a.m. every day and stay open until midnight. Diners sat on black vinyl-backed chairs around Formica tables or snagged a stool at the L-shaped counter. The Halls never needed to advertise. Word of mouth worked so well for them.

"Omaha's Black City Hall"

The restaurant did more than feed a community; it served as a meeting space for people to talk over issues. It earned the nickname "Omaha's Black City Hall," and key players in city and state politics were regularly spotted there, including Ernie Chambers, Brenda Council and Ben Gray. When redevelopment plans for North Omaha began to take shape, Dwight Johnson, a public affairs officer for the Omaha office of the Small Business Administration, headed to Fair Deal to get to know the key players in the area.

Council recalled dining at the restaurant in the 1960s as a young adult and the discussions among community activists. She learned a lot, but she said she really went there because the food was good: "It was like eating in your mother's kitchen. Mr. and Mrs. Hall were like community parents."

As the key meeting place in North Omaha, the restaurant also drew its share of celebrities. Ella Fitzgerald and the Reverend Jesse Jackson were said to have dined there. In O.J. Simpson's early days of professional football, he dined on greens and black-eyed peas with the late community leader Charles Washington.

Riots in North Omaha

In the late 1960s, the Near North Side riots badly hurt Twenty-Fourth Street. The first was on July 2, 1966.

"I stood on the corner one night during the riots and I cried. Business was never the same. We lost our white customers, and some blacks never came back. Whether they ever will, I don't know," a North Omaha business owner's wife told the *Omaha World-Herald*. Fair Deal Café was mostly spared and only had some smoke damage. Charlie called it luck.

While the riots adversely affected the neighborhood, most agreed the riots didn't entirely explain the area's downfall. Merchants allowed buildings to deteriorate or simply abandoned them. According to the *Omaha World-Herald*, "Between 1960 and 1990, nearly two people a day on average moved out of the area. One housing unit was destroyed every 2⅓ days, and one business or other non-housing unit disappeared every month."

While business closed in North Omaha, Fair Deal Café remained. After twenty years in business, customers could still sit down at the L-shaped counter and watch the black-and-white TV on top of the white refrigerator. While they waited for their food, they could still look at the different photo murals of soul food dishes hanging on the salmon-colored walls.

That's not to say it wasn't getting increasingly difficult for Charlie Hall to run his restaurant. There was a fire in 1972 that damaged the interior of the café. Small margins and the rising cost of food started making things difficult for Hall in that decade. Chitterlings, cooked pig intestines that had to be laboriously cleaned, used to cost him $0.49 for ten pounds back in the early days; in 1975, he had to pay $4.79 for the same amount.

Still, he insisted on keeping prices low. Meals were $1.40 to about $2.35 in the 1970s, and entrées consisted of meat with two vegetables served family style. On a good day, customers might find prime rib for $2.35. He would also serve up roast pork with brown gravy, dressing, cranberry sauce and candied yams for $2.05. On the low end, a meal of neck bones with cabbage, sliced tomatoes and onions was $1.40.

Hours were cut to help make ends meet. Fair Deal Café started closing on Mondays, and for the rest of the week, the restaurant closed at 6:00 p.m. It was an unfortunate fact of life that the restaurant needed to close that early each day. Charlie explained to the *Omaha World-Herald*: "Most of the robberies occur between 7 and 10 in the evening, and I'm afraid for my girls, so we get the hell out of here." The restaurant, though, had never been held up when he was interviewed in 1975, though it had been broken into.

The Fair Deal Café before the building was demolished. *Courtesy Omaha Economic Development Corporation.*

The interior of Fair Deal Café before the building was torn down. *Courtesy Omaha Economic Development Corporation.*

Business for North Omaha entrepreneurs continued to decline in the 1980s. But Charlie and his restaurant forged on, and the community thanked him for it. In 1986, he was honored for his work in business at the Mayor's Black Excellence Awards. In February 2000, he was honored for his contributions to the community; he had hired and helped more than six hundred high school students from the 1950s through the 1970s.

By the early 2000s, Charlie was approaching eighty. His step-grandson began to help out. He stopped making a menu, keeping just a small rotating selection of choices for his regulars who were in the know.

Charlie was eighty when he sold Fair Deal Café to Tamyra Wilson in 2002. It was Omaha's Near North Side's longest-running restaurant when it eventually closed in 2005 and was later demolished.

The Fair Deal Café was revived when a new restaurant opened in the same location in November 2016. *Author's collection.*

FAIR DEAL REVIVED

On November 30, 2016, Fair Deal Development was unveiled to the public at the same street corner where Fair Deal Café once sat. A new Fair Deal opened in the space and used some of the pieces of the old Fair Deal Café in its architecture and tables. The tin ceiling from the original space is in the dining room, bricks from the Halls' restaurant form the wall behind the bar and pieces of wood were used for tabletops and countertops.

"The Fair Deal Café will always be remembered as the heartbeat of this neighborhood," said Omaha mayor Jean Stothert during the ribbon-cutting ceremony.

Chapter 17

MISTER C'S

Year-Round Christmas Lights and Heaping Servings

There was no doubt that Mister C's made a lasting impression on every visitor. Few who passed through the quilted red leather doors could forget the year-round twinkling Christmas lights or the Sicilian diorama. Few could forget Mister C himself, Sebastiano "Yano" R. Caniglia.

The Mister C's that most remember came from a much humbler beginning. Long before there was an Italian-inspired plaza with a fountain, there was a drive-in. The year was 1952. Marshall's drive-in at 5319 North Thirtieth Street was for sale, and Yano Caniglia was looking to open his own restaurant. Though the place had running water, it had no drains. Still, Caniglia saw something there.

It took Caniglia one year to complete the renovations. The restaurant reopened as Caniglia's Royal Boy drive-in, with six stools, fifteen carhops and a two-thousand-light sign modeled after signs in Las Vegas. They served typical drive-in fare, including pizza burgers and steak burgers on homemade bread. In 1965, they served up a ten-cent burger special.

Royal Boy expanded in 1957 to allow more indoor seating. An appreciative boss, Caniglia recognized the top carhop each year by rewarding him or her with a new Studebaker.

It became Mister C's Steakhouse and Royal Boy in 1970.

The drive-in was the place to go for teenagers, especially after a date or prom. They weren't always the best of customers for Caniglia. Teens were known to steal his root beer mugs. Caniglia started marking the bottom of trays with the number of root beers ordered to make sure carhops got all the

The exterior of Caniglia's Royal Boy. *Courtesy the Caniglia family.*

Caniglia's Royal Boy and its carside service ended when Yano Caniglia opened Mister C's in its place in 1976. *Courtesy the Caniglia family.*

mugs back. But the kids caught on and replaced his tags with their own and made off with more than a few mugs.

Caniglia kept an eye on his teenage customers. Once, a car full of teenagers pulled into Royal Boy, innocently enough carrying some cherry cider from a local orchard. "Order, please," said a voice from the speaker. "Five cups of ice," said the driver. Mister C delivered the ice himself to make sure the beverage the teens were sipping met his approval.

The carside service ended in 1976, and the era of Mister C's began.

MISTER C'S EXPANSION

The restaurant that came to be known simply as Mister C's experienced tremendous expansion between 1976 and 1988. At its height, the restaurant expanded so much that Caniglia hired a full-time contractor. Some of the add-ons included the beautiful courtyard and garden, Piazza di Maria, named for Mrs. C and inspired by something Mister C saw at a circus headquarters.

Left: A nighttime view of Mister C's courtyard, the Piazza di Maria. *Courtesy Derek Eskens.*

Below: Yano Caniglia standing in the middle of the Piazza di Maria at Mister C's. *Courtesy the Durham Museum Photo Archive and* Omaha World-Herald.

At one point, there was talk of building a bridge and a lake with gondolas. Mrs. C nixed the ideas.

The restaurant grew so much that it could seat 1,400 people indoors and outdoors: 500 seats upstairs, 300 downstairs, 100 in the lounge and 500 outdoors.

ARRIVE WITH AN APPETITE

Like most of the restaurants run by members of the Caniglia family, Mister C's was known for large portions. Italian specialties included the traditional spaghetti dinner with meatballs or Italian sausage, lasagna casserole, chicken Parmesan, veal Parmesan and mancini chicken, which was grilled chicken topped with mozzarella cheese and Mister C's Italian peppers, along with pasta and Italian toast.

Other items on the menu included a range of meat specialties, like breaded veal and prime rib. There was plenty of steak on the menu, including a twenty-ounce Porterhouse that came with a salad, bread and a choice of potato.

Dinnertime at Mister C's. *Courtesy the Caniglia family.*

If there was still room for dessert, the customer favorite was Turtle Pie, with ice cream and praline filling. They also served Italian spumoni, Jell-O with whipped cream, cheesecake and ice cream.

WHAT PEOPLE REMEMBERED MOST

It's a tough call whether Mister C himself outshone his restaurant. A reporter described Caniglia in 1983: "If it was your first visit, you probably were still recovering from the dazzle of thousands of Christmas lights that festoon the place when he bustled up to your table, welcomed you in his booming voice and, if there were kids in your party, deftly twisted balloon animals for them."

It was a joy to be a child there. There was so much space for children to run around. And there was a balloon animal offered to every kid, and sometimes two for the birthday boy or girl. At Christmas, children were allowed to go upstairs to pick out a toy from the "toy room."

Restaurant regular Rhonda Wajda poses next to the little neighborhood inside Mister C's in December 2006. *Courtesy Rhonda Wajda.*

A dining room decorated with Christmas lights inside Mister C's. *Courtesy Derek Eskens.*

It's forgivable to think every visit to Mister C's was at Christmastime. The famous Christmas light decor started around 1971, when a waitress asked Caniglia to leave up the Christmas lights until her navy husband returned home. He returned that summer, but the lights stayed up. Permanently.

The lights inspired a poem that Mrs. C wrote in 1999; it was added to menus after that:

She begged Mister C to leave the lights burning,
until the time of her mate's returning.
Christmas was his favorite time of year,
and his journey for home was possibly near.
So up went the lights again as before,
and Mister C added a whole bunch more.
However, the sailor didn't return until June,
and for Mrs. C that wasn't too soon!
Christmas lights in summer, caused her to frown,
so she asked Mister C to take them down.
But by this time our customers fussed
that the year around lights should be a must.

The restaurant was festive, or kitschy, enough without the added shimmering lights. A glimpse around the dining room and you'd spot a pink

The exterior of Mister C's. *Courtesy Derek Eskens.*

neon "telefono" sign, stuffed animals, a faux parrot, some dangling plastic grapes. The *Omaha World-Herald* described it on its final day, September 30, 2006, as a 1970s time capsule: "The kaleidoscopic carpet of red, orange, yellow and black that covers the walls (still bright) and floors (muted from wear). The mirrors wherever the carpet is not. The quilted red-leather doors. The red-and-white-checked tablecloths. The black-steel frame chairs with orange vinyl seats."

For all its flair, it lacked one ingredient to keep it going: a successor to Mister C. Mister and Mrs. C were eighty-three when the decision was made to close the restaurant. Their children didn't want to keep the restaurant going; it was a lot of work to keep all the parts moving.

When Mister C's closed, it was like a funeral, complete with rain. Families dressed a little nicer than they should for Mister C's, and they walked a receiving line to talk to the owners and share pictures. A short video was played, making many tear up. A guest book was passed around.

A week later, equipment and memorabilia were auctioned off.

A bit of the nostalgia lives on in collectors' storage and private displays. A menu from the restaurant can be found on the administrative level of the W. Dale Clark Omaha Public Library Main branch location, which is not open to the public. A collection of Mister C's ties is on display at Hollywood Candy in Omaha's Old Market.

The restaurant's sweet marinara sauce is available in some grocery stores under the name of Mister C's.

Chapter 18

ODDO'S DRIVE-IN

Home of the Pookie Snackenberger and the Mo-She-Fro

Drive-ins enjoyed immense popularity in Omaha in the 1950s. Right in the thick of the craze, Irv Froydma pitched the idea of purchasing an old drive-in on North Thirtieth Street to his father-in-law, Anthony Oddo. Instead, Oddo suggested Froydma design one for them to build elsewhere, and in 1955, it became a reality: Oddo's Drive-In opened at 2410 South Thirteenth Street.

Oddo's was an all-brick building designed like classic drive-in restaurants, complete with bellhops delivering food to cars. Froydma said the early days of Oddo's Drive-In were so busy that they had to hire a police officer to maintain order and keep traffic moving.

The food was typical drive-in fare, like fried onion rings, spaghetti, shrimp and a lot of pizza. The restaurant was the first to serve broasted chicken in Omaha. Oddo's had to explain broasted chicken in advertisements, noting how it was "scientifically prepared" to be ready in five minutes.

They were known for their sandwiches, too, particularly because of the unique names given to them. There was the Pookie Snackenburger, which was inspired by a girl nicknamed Pookie, and the Mo-She-Fro made with two tenderloins and inspired by an old saying of Anthony Oddo's. Whenever he thought someone was stretching the truth, he'd say, "Don't give me that mo-she-fro."

A year after opening, Oddo had phones, called "Servus Fones," installed. Diners could order by phone from the table and parking area. It was new technology for the time, and Oddo's advertised itself as the first restaurant

Anthony Oddo, *at right*, dined with heavyweight boxing champion Rocky Marciano, *center*, who was in Omaha in 1954 for a Sons of Italy event. *Courtesy Irv Froydma.*

in the United States to have it. Oddo's also offered home delivery, which it called its "rolling oven."

The restaurant's dining room was remodeled in 1966. Air conditioning was put in and was a major selling point for Oddo's. To get people to come in and check it out, a promotion ran after the remodel giving away free spaghetti with every purchase of a tub of chicken. Tubs of chicken were ten or twenty pieces in a tub.

Froydma co-owned the restaurant with Oddo, with Froydma managing daily operations for thirteen years before he went on to another restaurant venture.

Oddo's Story

Oddo's past may have been the guiding force behind his generosity in adulthood. Oddo was one of the five original boys to live at Boys Town with Father Flanagan. He was fifteen when he was taken into Flanagan's first Home for the Boys located at Twenty-Fifth and Dodge Streets. Decades later, he said his "heart and soul" belonged to Boys Town. He was president of the Boys Town Association in 1953.

Oddo grew up to become a restaurateur in Omaha and became known for two things: his abundant generosity and his abundant appetite. He was affectionately known as the jolly fat man. He was always happy, and he explained that his weight was tied to his happiness. In 1967, he told a newspaper columnist simply, "I ate big when I was happy."

In his youth, he could get away with eating so much. He was a boxer back then, and he burned away the calories he ate. One time, in 1926, he won the Nebraska-Iowa hamburger eating championship by eating twenty-four hamburgers. In his older years, as owner of Oddo's Drive-In, a typical day's worth of food would be a breakfast of five eggs, bacon and eight to ten slices of toast. Lunch would be twelve or fifteen pork chops, plus another eight to ten slices of bread with butter. Dinner would be similar.

After one heart attack, the threat of another loomed, so in 1967, when he reached 400 pounds, he was ordered by doctors to lose weight. He lost more than 140 pounds. And his health improved with it.

Fire Strikes Oddo's Drive-In

Two years later, the restaurant was destroyed. A fire tore through Oddo's Drive-In on November 6, 1969. Suspected as arson, there was a huge explosion. One witness told the *Omaha World-Herald* that glass was flying everywhere. When Oddo arrived at the scene, a neighbor to the restaurant saw him weeping. The restaurant would never reopen.

Oddo retired following the fire. In spite of his improved health, he died from heart problems in 1974.

His generosity may have outshined his girth. When Oddo fell ill, the community rallied behind him. Columnist Wally Provost wrote in the *Omaha World-Herald* in 1974:

Dishing up pasta for a hungry reporter, spreading the good word about Boys Town, giving an ex-athlete a break, picking up tabs on the sly for down-and-outers, pitching in for favorite charities—that's the track record for our man Tony. The gang missed his cigar and big personality at the races this year. During his illness, there have been prayers for Tony from busboys and up to the archbishop level.

Chapter 19

ROSS' STEAK HOUSE

Why It Was Called One of America's Perfect Steak Restaurants

Ross' Steak House came from humble beginnings, but over the decades, it became an Omaha legend. It was named one of the "perfect steak" American restaurants. It was the place where celebrities dined. It started small but ended bigger than Ross Lorello probably could have ever imagined.

Lorello, a son of a Sicilian immigrant, started a small restaurant in downtown Omaha called Ross' Villa. That restaurant wasn't big enough for the vision Lorello had.

Omaha was expanding westward in the 1950s. The hub of activity was starting to migrate from downtown Omaha. In a few years, Seventy-Second Street would be the center of commerce and activities. Ahead of that trend, Lorello opened a restaurant much larger than his first. In 1956, Ross' Steak House was in the middle of a cornfield at 909 South Seventy-Second Street, but that didn't last long.

Ross' had the appearance of a traditional American steakhouse, dimly lit by chandeliers, with high ceilings, burgundy, brick and wood throughout. Each table had two tablecloths. It felt rich and inviting, and when people entered the dining room through the tall swinging doors, they truly made an entrance. If you didn't know the exact address, the giant neon Hereford's head out front served as a beacon.

In 1977, when the restaurant was enjoying its peak years, it was always busy. Even traditionally slow nights in Omaha were packed nights in the dining room of Ross'.

The exterior of Ross' Steak House at night in 1956. *Courtesy the Durham Museum Photo Archive.*

When you're in business for forty years, there's a good chance you'll have an odd story or two. Ross' might have one of Omaha's oddest. In 1966, chief bartender Fritz Johnson turned out to be an amnesiac. It was discovered that he was really Lawrence Bader of Akron, Ohio, who had a second wife and family.

THE PERFECT STEAK

The success of Ross' was due to a couple things. First and probably foremost was the food. It was more than good. It stood out nationally. *Esquire* magazine once called it one of the "perfect steak" American restaurants, and *Dining* magazine listed it as one of America's top one hundred restaurants in 1973. It earned the Silver Butterknife Award and the Omaha Hospitality Hall of Fame. The Nebraska Restaurant Association named Ross' Restaurant of the Year in 1992.

Lorello knew beef. He was known to buy Ak-Sar-Ben grand champion steers for his restaurant and never used tenderizer on them. The high-quality steak sold for $2.95 for a filet mignon and $3.95 for the "famous cut" of prime rib in the beginning.

Ross' served other fine foods, including lobster tail, Ross' famous lasagna and broiled lamb chops. They made a mean martini, as well. For ninety-five cents, a patron could order Ross' famous king-sized martini.

The restaurant drew fans from beyond Omaha. Stockyard owners from Yankton, South Dakota, dined at Ross' for thirty years. They were particular about their beef, being owners of stockyards in two states and all. "We're connoisseurs of good beef," Gail Sohler told the *Omaha World-Herald* on one of the restaurant's final days. "We've always been particular. That's why we picked this place." His wife explained that they were just kids when they started dining there. "The good old-fashioned steakhouses are going to be hard to find now."

Location was also a key point for Ross'. It may have been built on the edge of town, but over time, Seventy-Second Street became a major destination. Ross' location eventually became known as "the strip," with the world-famous Nebraska Furniture Mart on it. Its proximity to Ak-Sar-Ben Race Track and Coliseum meant it regularly drew winners and losers after the races.

It could be said that Ross himself was another reason the restaurant was so successful. He had a saying: "Every day is a gift."

Running Ross' Steak House was a dream for him. His daughter Sandra said, "It represents the American dream. My dad's father came over from Sicily, and dad opened Ross' Villa downtown on Thirteenth

A postcard from Ross' Steak House with a picture of Mr. and Mrs. Ross Lorello. *Author's collection.*

Street—a smaller place—then came out here to be his own boss and to make people happy."

He succeeded in spreading the happiness. Lorello was winner of the City of Hope's "Great Guy" Award in 1978.

Celebrity Sightings

If you dined at Ross', there was always a good chance you'd spot someone famous. Among the notables were Jimmy Durante, Bob Hope, Perry Como, Frank Sinatra, Henry Mancini, Mel Torme, Liberace, Jack Benny, Liza Minnelli, June Allyson, Danny Thomas, Robert Goulet, Florence Henderson, Pat Boone and Kim Novak. The list goes on.

The Lorellos remember serving Mitzi Gaynor, Louis Prima, Rocky Marciano, Desi Arnaz, Barbara Eden, Joel McCrea, Ed McMahon and Jim Nabors. Politicians like the Kennedys (Jack, Robert and Ted), as well as presidential candidate George Wallace, have dined there, as well as famous athletes including Arnold Palmer and Joe DiMaggio. Actor Robert Taylor, a Nebraska native, was a regular there.

The Lorellos' daughter Sandra told the *Omaha World-Herald* about her favorite celebrity sighting at Ross': "My favorite when I was young was Red Skelton, who was absolutely wonderful. He made balloons and insisted on going into the kitchen to joke around—then had dinner with Mom and Dad."

Going Out on Top

The 1995 closing of Ak-Sar-Ben Race Track and Coliseum hit businesses in the area hard. Ross' Steak House was no exception. Sandra, who'd taken over the business after her father and brother passed away and her mother retired, was the restaurant's final owner. She explained that in the end, she couldn't have someone else run Ross'. "We're going out on top, and I want to thank from the bottom of my heart the people of Omaha who have been so good to us over the years."

The restaurant closed in November 1996.

The property was sold to Lerner Company, and today the retail chain Kohl's has a store on the site.

Chapter 20

TROVATO'S LOUNGE

A Dundee Neighborhood Original

Trovato's Lounge had a half-century-long run as a Dundee neighborhood mainstay, but it almost didn't happen.

The Italian eatery opened at 5013 Underwood Avenue on April 30, 1956. Four days later, a fire severely damaged the building. Then, a month later, there was an attempted break-in. It was a rough start, but owners John and Rena Trovato had it back in business by June.

Trovato's was located in a recessed building off the main street of the charming Dundee neighborhood. If you weren't a regular—most customers turned into one—you would likely try to enter the restaurant through what appeared to be the entrance. A 1989 food critic joked you could always spot the newcomer:

> *The novice first tries what looks like the logical access—the architect's office next door to the actual entrance, which has a green awning above the door. Then the new guy looks a bit put off by the small wine-laden package store area straight ahead and the tavern look to his left. Trovato's small dining room actually is in the rear and usually is as stuffed as the homemade ravioli and cannelloni during dinner hours.*

Divided into two main dining rooms and two smaller rooms, the atmosphere at Trovato's was subdued and sophisticated, with low lighting, red flocked wallpaper and wood paneling. On certain nights, patrons could listen to live music while they dined.

The restaurant served a variety of American and classical Italian dishes, like lasagna and several types of fettuccine. The Trovatos were, after all, Italian immigrants. The menu boasted many handmade items that were time-consuming to prepare, including gnocchi served with a meat sauce and chopped sirloin meatballs for $1.95 and their specialty, ravioli stuffed with chicken for $2.25. Italian entrées came with minestrone soup, an antipasto plate, tossed salad, bread and coffee or tea. Italian desserts included spumoni or bisque tortoni for $0.30 and cannoli for $0.35.

The thin crust pizza was popular in the 1980s and continued to grow in popularity into the 2000s. The restaurant also served a veal Parmesan that continued to live on after the restaurant had closed—the now-closed second incarnation of Italian Gardens prepared it using the same recipe as well.

The Trovatos retired in March 1981, selling the restaurant to Bill Beeler and two partners. Over the next two decades, the restaurant switched hands several times, with John Coolidge selling the location to the final owner, Jeff Camp, in September 2006.

TROVATO'S SWAN SONG

Trovato's had been struggling when Camp assumed ownership; it was losing about $3,000 a month. The kitchen had started to stray from the handwritten recipes of Rena Trovato, as they were too time-consuming to prepare. Camp kept the Trovato's menu from before but resumed Rena's methods of preparation and upgraded the food purchased for the restaurant.

Business started to turn around. Some nights, people would be lined up at 5:00 p.m. waiting for the restaurant to open. Trovato's was once again filled with conversations and the hustle and bustle of a wait staff trying to move a lot of dishes out of a tiny kitchen.

The restaurant's bar was a hot spot after dining hours ended. Live music played on Thursday, Friday and Saturday nights. Camp said once the restaurant closed for the night, the bar would be packed and the crowd would overflow into the parking lot.

One Sunday night, one of the restaurant's regulars, Susie Buffett, caused a stir at Trovato's. Buffett, the philanthropist daughter of billionaire Warren Buffett, arrived just before service was ending. In her group was U2's lead singer, Bono. There was no prior warning of their arrival, said Camp, but it didn't matter; they served the group, and the staff had fun meeting a celebrity. Word spread that he was in the neighborhood, and onlookers arrived to get a glimpse. Since it was technically bar hours, families could not enter, so they stayed out front. By the time the group left, Camp said there were about 150 people pressed up against the window looking in.

After two years, it started to be a challenge keeping dishes at a price point customers could accept. Back in 1989, there was some uncertainty about nudging prices past ten dollars. Camp admitted that in 2008, it was difficult keeping prices under twenty dollars since the cost of veal shank had risen to twenty-eight dollars a pound. Prices had to be raised to bring them in line with rising food costs, and he adjusted staffing for better efficiency.

It only prolonged the inevitable. Camp filed for Chapter 11 bankruptcy protection in March 2008. A dispute with the property owner, D.C. "Woody" Brandford, sealed the restaurant's fate. Camp said Brandford objected to the bankruptcy proceedings. Brandford said he objected to Camp not filing a reorganization plan.

After fifty-two years in the Dundee neighborhood, Trovato's closed on July 27, 2008. The building has been home to various restaurants since 2008, including Agave. It's now Avoli Osteria, a northern Italian restaurant.

Chapter 21

ELI CANIGLIA'S VENICE INN

For Celebrity Spotting or Celebrating a Win at Ak-Sar-Ben Race Track, Head to the Venice Inn

Caniglia family members operated many restaurants across Omaha, but it was Eli Caniglia's Venice Inn at 6920 Pacific Street that had the storied history of attracting celebrities along with serving up Italian steakhouse fare. Some entertained onstage in the Cascade Lounge. Some stopped by for a juicy steak after performing at the nearby Ak-Sar-Ben Race Track and Coliseum. Having worked at the restaurant since the beginning at ages ten and twelve with their dad, Chuck and Jerry Caniglia had a lot of encounters with stars. "That was the heyday," Jerry Caniglia told the *Omaha World-Herald* in 2014. "It was the most fun, after those Ak-Sar-Ben shows, for a 16-year-old kid."

*****

Nuncio "Eli" Caniglia opened Venice Inn on August 14, 1957, at a prime location. Well, all signs pointed to it becoming a prime location, at least. There was still corn growing across the street from the restaurant. But in short time, the Seventy-Second Street corridor would turn into the city's newest retail and dining destination, and a few blocks away, the Ak-Sar-Ben Coliseum would start drawing in world-class entertainers.

There was a lot of fanfare for the opening night. A huge ad in the newspaper the day before invited people to be a "first-nighter" at the formal opening of the restaurant. The ad touted the spacious dining area, steaks and perfectly mixed drinks by skilled mixologists. On opening night, an

The exterior of Eli Caniglia's Venice Inn. *Courtesy Matt Johnson.*

accordion player entertained diners in a space that had the charming look of an Italian trattoria.

Things did not continue on a charmed path for Venice Inn. The day after the restaurant opened, construction started on a new bridge over Little Papio Creek. The result was a ten-month-long closure of Pacific Street right in front of the restaurant.

Chuck Caniglia said it was a rough period for his dad. The bridge's repeated closure over the years, according to Jerry Caniglia, continually created restricted access to the restaurant, making the first fifteen years a struggle.

VENICE INN'S BEST DAYS

At its height of popularity in the 1960s and '70s, the swanky steakhouse was packed nightly. Brick walls and low lighting helped to create a grotto-like atmosphere. There was a neighborly buzz in the air. Italian standards like Puccini or Louis Prima played on the speakers in the background.

Venice Inn served up many dishes from old family recipes, many going back to Sicily. The marinara was sweet, and steak was proudly all USDA Choice and, as they like to note in the 1980s, "Nebraska corn-fed beef."

The dining room of Eli Caniglia's Venice Inn with the buffet table on the right. *Courtesy Matt Johnson.*

The restaurant served a chateaubriand for two for $9.50, which included a small bottle of wine. Non-steak offerings included chicken dishes like chicken cacciatore and seafood entrées like salmon steak and Rocky Mountain trout. Those entrées came with soup; choice of spaghetti or mostaccioli; choice of French fries, baked potato or hash browns; salad; freshly baked Italian bread; and coffee or tea. Even the heartiest eaters had trouble finishing.

Popular Italian dishes were the veal and chicken Parmesan. The Canigilias had a few specialties of their own on the menu, including the spaghetti a la Caniglia entrée, which was topped with chicken livers, and Eli's special Italian sausage with spaghetti. There were eighteen different types of pizza available to order, with traditional toppings like pepperoni and more unique offerings like potatoes, tuna fish or shrimp. Hamburger pizza came with the option of single crust or double crust. The Friday Super Pizza was topped with mushrooms, shrimp, pimiento, green peppers and onions. It was made in two sizes: $1.75 for a small or $2.50 for a large.

Venice Inn's house-made liver pâté in the salad bar was the stuff of legends. Some would eat it spread on a warm roll with butter.

On Stage in the Cascade Lounge

The Cascade Lounge at Venice Inn got its name from the indoor waterfall. The lounge, with its sunken bar, was the place to go for comedy shows in the restaurant's heyday. Dan Rowan and Dick Martin of *Rowan & Martin's Laugh-In* performed on stage, as did George Gobel from *The George Gobel Show* and the comedic violinist Henny Youngman. In the 1980s, musical entertainment started to phase out the comedians. Local performers like Johnny Ray Gomez would perform multi-night runs there. In the mid-'80s, Venice Inn began to have live music just on Friday and Saturday nights.

Venice Inn had a lot of high-profile diners, especially in the 1960s and '70s. Those in the know headed to the Venice Inn's lounge after a big-name comic performed at the Coliseum; there was a good chance you'd spot them there. Joey Bishop from the Rat Pack sipped a drink there, and entertainer George Kirby ate a meal there.

Eli and the Caniglia Family Values

Eli Caniglia learned how to run a restaurant by working at his family's business, Original Caniglia's Pizzaria and Steakhouse. Call it the "School of Caniglia." They knew how to treat customers, and the pizzeria started the basic principle of the family's many establishments that followed: serve good food at a good price, and lots of it. Eli was the second of the Caniglia family to open his own place away from the Original Caniglia's at Seventh and Pierce Streets. Yano Caniglia (Mister C's) was the first. At one point, the Caniglias had a hand in running eight restaurants around Omaha.

Eli's presence was huge at Venice Inn. On Saturday nights, his sons would remember him inspecting every plate leaving the kitchen. He was great with children, and his sons have had customers tell them they remember their dad rewarding them with a candy bar if they finished their spaghetti. Eli worked at Venice Inn even while battling cancer. He worked there right up until the end—two months before he passed away on September 6, 1983.

Eli made sure his sons worked their way up from the bottom. Jerry and Chuck started as busboys and moved up to the unpretentious jobs, including dishwashers, pizza cooks and bartenders. They learned every aspect of the business before becoming partners with their father in about 1973. They took over after Eli died.

CHANGING TIMES IN THE 1970S AND BEYOND

Live horse racing started in the 1970s at Ak-Sar-Ben. It helped the restaurant's business in the beginning, and in 1988, it still occasionally helped on weekends. In the late spring of 1988, they'd still serve about 500 to 750 diners on a Friday or Saturday night. Jerry said his dad would run "winner" and "loser" steak specials. Those with losing tickets from the Ak-Sar-Ben Race Track got bigger steaks than the winners.

The track, however, hurt the Venice Inn's business more than it helped it. Chuck said when the horse races went to a 4:00 p.m. start time in 1988, business dropped 15 to 30 percent. Then, the dog track opened, and business dropped another 10 to 15 percent. Party rentals made up for the losses, at least.

The *Omaha World-Herald* would regularly run restaurant round-ups for out-of-towners headed to the racetrack. A not-so-enthusiastic mention of Venice Inn led to the reviewer being invited to return and try it again. Ultimately, the reviewer conceded that the dishes were done well but only mildly seasoned. The reviewer noted that the Caniglias know their customers, and their customers prefer "the home-brewed red sauce, which is on the sweet side and low on herbs and spices. Omahans tend to prefer garlic sauces that only hint of garlic."

A dining room at Eli Caniglia's Venice Inn. *Courtesy Matt Johnson.*

Members of the Mancuso family celebrated Sandy Mancuso's birthday at Eli Caniglia's Venice Inn for about ten years before the restaurant closed. *Courtesy Christine Dostal.*

In spite of the occasional snarky review, loyal customers continued to frequent Venice Inn in the 1980s and 1990s. The restaurant expanded, adding a terrace and party room. What started out seating 100 people in the dining room and 50 in the lounge grew to fit 465 in 1987.

As it was in the beginning, the quantity of food served didn't change. There was still a large variety of Italian dishes to choose from beyond the mostaccioli and lasagna fare, including shrimp and scallop fettuccine ($8.75), eggplant Parmesan ($7.25), chicken Parmesan ($7.50) and chicken tetrazzini ($8.50).

One reviewer recalled dining in 1985 and pointed out that it was hard to enjoy entrées because by the time they arrived, she wasn't hungry anymore. Diners always started with the salad bar and then went on to enjoy the soup, such as the broccoli cheese. Appetizers would come to the table after that. For entrées, she and her dinner date opted for the Italian fiesta, which included mostaccioli, ravioli, a hot and spicy sausage, sautéed peppers, a hefty portion of baked tufoli ("a yummy manicotti stuffed with hamburger and mozzarella and drenched in the restaurant's flavorful tomato sauce"), a wedge of salami and Provolone cheese and a meatball. Then she had Italian spumoni for dessert.

The beef was customers' clear favorite. In the 1980s, there were six meaty options on the menu ranging from a twenty-ounce T-bone for $11.95 to a ten-ounce top sirloin club for $8.25, as well as a chateaubriand ($22.50 for two) and the filet and lobster or crab leg combinations ($17.50). The chateaubriand stayed on the menu through the years, creeping up in price to go with the times. It cost $28.95 for two in 1992; in 2002, it was $43.95.

In 2011, head chef Al Bonge III shared the secret (most of it, at least) to Venice Inn's great steaks. He'd worked at the restaurant since he was fifteen, working as a busboy in 1978. The secret, as he explained to the *Omaha World-Herald*:

> *We buy beef from a couple companies, mostly Omaha Steaks. We buy the loin and cut whatever you want. It takes practice. I cut several kinds of steaks every day. We have slow-roasted prime rib, too. On the cheaper side: the top sirloin is very good. All our meat is dry-aged. We take it out of the package and let it age in the cooler. It helps improve flavor. It gives an age to the meat. Otherwise it's going to be a little tougher and less flavorful. We have our own seasonings that we put on our steaks. It's unique. I can't tell you how we make it.*

CANIGLIAS IN THE SPOTLIGHT

The Caniglia family continued on for two more decades, serving up quality food to Italian steakhouse fans, and they were recognized for their efforts. Chuck Caniglia was named Omaha Restaurateur of the Year in 2005.

In 2010, Venice Inn had a moment in the national spotlight. The Travel Channel show *Food Wars* pitted Venice Inn's New York strip against the steak from another local restaurant, Piccolo Pete's. The angle? The restaurants were owned by cousins. In true reality TV form, producers tried to get the cousins to bad mouth the other. But they couldn't. It was still a must-watch show for Omahans who are characteristically loyal to one particular steakhouse.

Venice Inn won with its prime New York strip. The menus were changed to add the description: "Caniglia's signature award-winning Prime New York Strip, Travel Channel's *Food Wars*' winner."

For some time, the *Food Wars* exposure brought in a new generation to Venice Inn. Many first-timers who visited following the episode had lived in Omaha their entire lives and admitted to not knowing about the restaurant until the show aired.

More than fifty years after Venice Inn opened, and nearly twenty years after the Coliseum closed, the restaurant shuttered its doors on May 3, 2014. Prior to closing, Chuck and Jerry speculated they'd be the last Caniglias to run the restaurant, hinting that another party might take over the restaurant one day. Instead, they received an offer they couldn't refuse. The land was a hot commodity largely due to the renaissance happening where the Coliseum once stood. A multi-use development called Aksarben Village was breathing new life into the area.

The building was unceremoniously razed after its purchase, and today, an empty lot remains.

Chapter 22

TODD'S DRIVE-IN

Omaha's Official Teen Hangout in the 1960s

Back in the 1960s, cruising Dodge Street became a thing. "Cruising" involved teenagers driving the stretch of the main thoroughfare, spotting friends, making eyes with someone new and hanging out at drive-ins.

On the quintessential loop were Todd's Drive-In and Dining Room and Tiner's Drive-In. Todd's was the place to be for a generation. *Esquire* magazine asked teens to write in telling the editors where the official hangout was in their hometown. Todd's won the poll and was deemed the official Omaha teen hangout.

At its peak in 1968, 1,500 cars were served on Todd's busiest nights of the week.

*****

The drive-in concept—mixing cars, youth and fast food—was fairly new in Omaha when Steve Urosevich opened Todd's Drive-In. Urosevich, a son of Serbian immigrant packinghouse workers, had been in Southern California and saw how it attracted teens. So on May 23, 1958, he converted his father-in-law's restaurant into a drive-in, installing indoor seating and three outdoor drive-in stalls. Located at 7720 Dodge Street, it was on the outskirts of town.

The timing was perfect. Teens had unprecedented access to cars and more free time than they knew what to do with. The year Todd's opened was the height of the drive-in craze, when the novelty of eating in your car was new to everyone. Everyone was excited for carhops to deliver trays of hot hamburgers and golden fries to their car windows.

Todd's Drive-In was so well received that eighty-four stalls were eventually added and indoor seating expanded to seventy. Car stalls had electronic speakers for customers to place their orders. Teenage carhops delivered the meals to vehicles. The drive-in served typical drive-in fare: hamburgers, fries and fifteen-cent malts.

During the day, a cross-section of the city dined there. Construction workers to businessmen ordered the twenty-five-cent tacos, foot-long hot dogs and burgers. The popular Todd Burger was sixty-five cents. Pizza was also on the menu. An entire sausage pizza was ninety-five cents.

On Sundays, Todd's sold the popular Tom Thumb donuts, a dozen silver dollar–sized donuts. They cost twenty cents.

Teens, Their Hot Cars and Todd's

Much like Mel's Diner in the movie *American Graffiti*, Todd's was a hot spot to show off hot cars for teens. A typical Saturday night would involve youth "cruising the strip" or "driving the loop" between Todd's at Seventy-Seventh and Dodge Streets and Tiner's Drive-In at Forty-Fourth and Dodge Streets.

Recalling those days, Mike Devereaux told the *Omaha World-Herald*, "If you were not lucky enough to get space at Todd's or Tiner's, you kept making loops. We put a lot of miles on those cars."

With so many young drivers on the road, there were bound to be accidents, unfortunately. In 1960, emergency vehicles raced east on Dodge

Traffic on Dodge Street in 1968. A sign for Todd's Drive-In is on the left side of the road. *Courtesy the Durham Museum Photo Archive and* Omaha World-Herald.

Street, sirens wailing and lights flashing. Everyone knew something bad had happened. According to the *Omaha World-Herald*:

> *After football games on one October night, a group of teens cruising the loop were riding in a car that turned into Elmwood Park at 11:30 p.m. The car struck a tree at high speed and six teenagers were killed. Investigators suspected drag racing, but witnesses never came forward to identify another vehicle. Dodge Street itself was busy and closely watched, and nothing remotely similar ever happened on the actual Dodge loop.*

Decades later, it was still believed to be the deadliest auto accident in the city's history.

Rowdiness—especially after certain high school sporting events—was not uncommon at Todd's, though it was quickly dealt with. There were always a couple off-duty police officers around to keep the peace. Urosevich respected his young customers, but he didn't tolerate much. He reported underage drinking and serious fighting. He was known to contact schools and coaches if a perpetrator played on a team. He even contacted parents. "I'd send a certified letter to the parents, telling them their child was not allowed back until they came over to meet with me," he once told the *Omaha World-Herald*.

For the most part, though, the atmosphere was jovial at Todd's during its best days. At the height of Todd's, teens crowded the restaurant at night. They'd go to meet their friends and, maybe, fall in love. That was the case for Harry and Julie Wilson, who met at Todd's in 1966. Harry was new to town, recently stationed at Offutt Air Force Base. Julie had graduated Benson High just a year earlier. They made eye contact as he was driving his midnight blue 1964 Chevy Impala and she was in the driver's seat of her red 1965 Ford Mustang. After a year-long courtship, the two married. Harry told the *Omaha World-Herald* he felt blessed to have spotted that cute girl in the Mustang on that August night. "The best day of my life was when I met her," he said.

Fast Food Edges Out the Drive-ins

As much as it was the place to be seen for baby boomers and their hot rods, it didn't remain that way. Rumors swirled that there was a drug problem there, and parents complained.

For a while, Urosevich defended the drive-in, saying a few were ruining it for the majority. He insisted youth needed more places to hang out, not fewer.

In the 1960s, fast-food restaurants began to gain popularity, edging out drive-ins in a competitive market to draw rushed diners. Todd's Drive-In was located in a prime spot, and two franchises approached Urosevich.

Urosevich announced the drive-in would close to "reorganize" in November 1969. He declined to elaborate at the time, but the newspaper noted that the owner had purchased a permit to build a car wash. When Todd's closed for good, Urosevich told the newspaper the drive-in still did good business.

Ultimately, the building was razed and kitchen supplies were auctioned off. The car wash never happened.

Today, the property is leased to Burger King.

Chapter 23

GAS LAMP RESTAURANT AND LOUNGE

A Mainstay on Top 20 Restaurant Lists in the 1960s and 1970s, Largely Due to Prime Rib

In a city known for beef, having a reputation for serving the best cut of steak guaranteed longevity in the restaurant business. No doubt that would have been the case for the Firmature family's Gas Lamp Restaurant and Lounge, which reigned throughout the 1960s and '70s, if it weren't for one fateful winter morning.

The Gas Lamp, located at 3006 Leavenworth Street, specialized in prime rib. The menu explained: "All prime rib prepared in a special and secret manner developed in and known only to the Gas Lamp." The Diamond Jim Brady cut, weighing in at twenty-four ounces, was $7.95, versus $5.75 for the English cut or $6.95 for the Gas Lamp cut.

In 1979, an *Omaha World-Herald* restaurant reviewer said the prime rib was in a class by itself: "I haven't found its peer anywhere, and it's served in an elegant atmosphere—I prefer the front room for intimacy."

The reviewer, Peter Citron, had never made a top twenty list of Omaha restaurants without including Gas Lamp, and he had spent years dining at Omaha's best restaurants. He wrote, "The reason is simple: Firmatures offers fine prime rib at a remarkable price in a lovely Victorian setting and with a well-rounded wine menu."

The prime rib's flavor, another reviewer noted later, was "all beef, nothing added or subtracted."

"You Won't Eat Better Steaks"

The Firmature brothers—Jay, Bob and Ernie—opened the restaurant in 1961. This wasn't the first, nor the last, restaurant run by the family, but it was one that garnered national attention. The restaurant was recognized for excellence by *Holiday* magazine two years in a row; few restaurants in Nebraska made the cut each year. In the July 1969 issue, the magazine noted, "You won't eat better steaks in Omaha." The accolades continued in the July–August 1970 issue, when the magazine stated the Gas Lamp continued "the great steak tradition of Omaha in a beautiful setting."

It was all about the details that made the dining experience so memorable. Serving only dinner, it was a place to impress your guests, with fine table linens, china and exquisite tableware. It was a quiet, refined place to dine, with deeply cushioned booths in the dining room. Most men wore coats and ties to dine there. The *Omaha World-Herald* wrote in 1980, "It's a restaurant to entertain your boss, treat a parent or spouse on their birthday, or impress the new love of your life."

Beef would always be the featured entrée, but it wasn't its only special dish. The variety of specialties was one of the Gas Lamp's appeals. The chef served up dishes with sauces that were unusual for that time in Omaha, notably the duck in orange sauce. All entrées included an appetizer for the table consisting of a tray of liver pâté, corn relish, pickled beets, garbanzo beans and chilies.

Wine connoisseurs appreciated the proper wine service at the restaurant. Wine was served by the captain, who would present the cork to the host of the table and pour him the first glass to sample. The practice wasn't too common for the time. The wine list was extensive, and the prices were also reasonable.

The Gas Lamp sat 104 people, and if dining on the weekends, you had to plan ahead and make a reservation. One New Year's Eve, Ernie Firmature boldly told the local newspaper that the festive night would be like any other Saturday night at the restaurant, crowd-wise.

Live Entertainment at the Gas Lamp

In its early days, the Gas Lamp had live music almost nightly. For five years, the ornate Gold Coast Lounge was the site of long-running entertainment.

Performers were usually booked for a six-week stint, before it was cut in half in 1965 to allow for more variety.

The Firmatures booked a lot of top-notch performers, many who skewed toward ragtime music. Some of the performers to have played the lounge were Bob Darch, Ragtime Ray Rose, Dale Linville, Harry White, Ben Jack, Ragtime Dollar Bill and Norma Payne. The audience would sip drinks in the classy lounge, with mirrors on the walls, Victorian-style red brocade wallpaper and red velvet furniture.

Gary Ellison was the last ragtime performer to tickle the ivories in the lounge on November 5, 1966. At the time, Ernie Firmature said piano bars were on the way out and it was getting harder to book good pianists. In 1967, the owner hinted at a return of live music but said whatever they'd choose, it wouldn't be ragtime. "We wore ragtime piano out here. Besides, it's just not the thing for this room," Ernie told the *Omaha World-Herald*.

THE END OF DIAMOND JIM?

On a chilly February morning in 1980, a three-alarm fire broke out in the Gas Lamp. The restaurant and lounge were heavily damaged by the flames, smoke and water. In the early hours of February 6, firefighters worked to extinguish the blaze, as ice began to form on the scene. When the smoke cleared, the building had been gutted.

Police initially expected arson. The building was a total loss and was eventually razed. At first, Ernie Firmature said the restaurant would be rebuilt, but in the end, the property was sold. It took a year and a half to sell the property after the fire.

Once the restaurant closed, one of the Firmatures' other restaurants, the Sidewalk Café in Regency Court, continued to serve the prime rib, along with several other popular dishes. While the Diamond Jim was not on the menu, Jim Firmature hinted that you could get it if you just asked.

Chapter 24

PROM TOWN HOUSE

Once at the Hub of City Life, the Home to Several Popular Bars and Restaurants Was Destroyed by Tornado

The demise of the Prom Town House overshadowed the food and experience of dining there.

The address 7000 Dodge Street has always been the location of a hotel. Town House Motor Hotel was first in the space before the national hotel chain Prom Motor Hotel Inc. purchased the building and restaurant in 1963, adding Prom to the name.

The hotel was large, with 450 rooms, dining facilities like the Hawaiian Room and 5 cocktail lounges that included the Town Pump and the Piano Lounge.

Pat Gobel was a young man when he worked at the Observatory lounge at the Prom Town House, and he recalled the popularity of the hotel's many restaurants and bars in a 2013 interview in *Food & Spirits*: "The Prom Townhouse was the bomb. Back in the day, if you wanted to go out, that was the place to go. They had a really good Japanese restaurant, a really good mainline restaurant, and a good Chinese restaurant all in one place."

Location helped draw in celebrities like Don Knotts and Casey Stengel. Many businesses were built near the intersection of Seventy-Second and Dodge Streets, and the area had become the center of town, the place to be.

The hotel's name changed again in October 1974 to Downtowner Motor Inn when another national chain—the Nashville-based Downtowner-Rowntowner Motor Inns—purchased the building. The chain ran seventy

A postcard for the Town House, which was renamed Prom Town House after a change of ownership. *Courtesy Larry Richling.*

locations, and Omaha's was its largest. It was confusing for travelers, though. With a name like Downtowner, visitors expected to be in a hotel in downtown Omaha. Regardless, the owners thought it was a fitting name, and it stuck.

Downtowner Motor Inn didn't have a long run at its location, though.

THE TORNADOES OF 1975

On the afternoon of May 6, 1975, at least two tornadoes ripped through Omaha. The Downtowner was destroyed. It was considered by some to be the worst tornado since the Easter Sunday tornado in 1913. The scene at the hotel was described in the *Omaha World-Herald* as being surrounded by overturned cars. "In roofless motel rooms, furniture was jumbled and all kinds of debris—corrugated steel, concrete, brick, lumber and glass—were strewn in all directions."

After the tornado, a seafood restaurant called Nelson's Landing was built on the site. Many businesses came and went in that area, including a Blockbuster, Bombay Bicycle Club and a Brock Residence Inn (then owned by Marriott). The site now has an extended-stay hotel, as well as a strip mall and OfficeMax.

Chapter 25

JACK HOLMES' GROUND COW

The Sauce Is What Made These Hamburgers Stand Out

Jack Holmes' Ground Cow was known for one thing: burgers. The deluxe six-ounce juicy hamburgers at Ground Cow were the stuff of legend.

In 1997—twenty years after the restaurant closed—readers wrote in to the *Omaha World-Herald* sharing what they thought made "Omahans Omahans," finishing the phrase "You're so Omaha if..." One reader answered with "You're so Omaha if you go to a place called the Ground Cow for a fancy dinner."

Ground Cow was not a fancy place by any stretch of the imagination. But in a city proud of its beef, if you served a good burger, you were popular.

*****

Jack Holmes started Ground Cow after a brief stint in retirement. The restaurateur had returned to Omaha after serving in World War II and opened the Jack Holmes Steak House. He closed it in 1962, ready for retirement. But he wasn't finished. He was only fifty, after all. And he was itching to get back into the restaurant game.

In 1964, Holmes opened Jack Holmes' Ground Cow at 7425 Pacific Street.

"He wanted to open a family restaurant," his son, Dr. T.J. Holmes, said years later, after his father passed away. "One of the reasons he retired from the steakhouse business was because of the late hours. He got the idea of opening up a restaurant that catered more to families with hamburgers and ribs."

Holmes managed to serve up the perfect hamburger, in spite of the fact that he actually hated hamburgers. It was that hatred that inspired one key thing behind Ground Cow's success: the sauces on the deluxe burgers. Holmes doused his burgers with sauce so that he'd eat them. The Elegant Olly, for instance, was covered in bearnaise sauce. Other burgers were topped with a Hawaiian sauce, mushroom gravy and others.

Things went so well that Ground Cow had to move to a larger location in 1971—just a block over to 7555 Pacific Street.

Ground Cow's big, blue bold lettering stated "fresh ground cow," in case you weren't sure what the burgers were made out of. Sandwiches had interesting names: Olly's Upper Crust, Croissant Delight, Monsieur Reuben and French Connection. The fries at Ground Cow had fans, too. Diners would order heaping servings of Husker Fries.

Though Holmes didn't want to work late hours, he always wanted to be at his restaurants, and that didn't change with Ground Cow. After fourteen years of being ever-present, Holmes ended Ground Cow's marveled run on Pacific Street. At sixty-six, Holmes was ready to retire for good in 1978. That year, he sold the Ground Cow. It eventually closed in December 1980.

The Mexican restaurant Fernando's on Pacific is now where Ground Cow used to be.

Chapter 26

FRENCH CAFÉ

The Romantic Restaurant That Helped Revive the Old Market

The French Café was a special place for Omahans, with a romantic ambiance that made it the ideal setting for marriage proposals or prom dates.

For the city, though, the restaurant served another important duty: it was one of the key players of the revitalization of the Old Market in the 1970s. In the 1960s, the Old Market was a decaying neighborhood. The rundown area was described as the city's "nearest approach to Baghdad." Many had already declared it beyond saving. One man announced that the "Omaha City Market is dead."

But another man had a lofty vision. Sam Mercer, a native of Omaha and an attorney in Paris, announced in January 1968 that he intended to revive the Old Market. Owning most of the property in the area, he set to restoring the buildings. The buildings had all been built in the 1880s and 1890s, so Mercer decided the restoration process had to retain the look of the buildings. A year after the proposal announcement, twelve businesses were added. Where the Galinsky Fruit Company once operated from 1906 to 1941, the area's crown jewel opened: the French Café. The building was slated for demolition when Mercer and his friend Cedric Hartman acquired it.

Mercer and Hartman renovated what once was a dirty warehouse into an inviting, pristine restaurant while managing to retain many of the essential aspects of the Galinsky Fruit Company. Mercer simply said they managed to keep things recognizable because "we borrowed no money and spent very little but all our own." They learned later the best way to renovate old buildings was to change as little as possible and leave well enough alone.

The Allure of the French

The French Café opened at 1017 Howard Street in early February 1969. On staff at the opening were Parisian chef Toussaint Moallic and his wife, Apollo Faison, a former nightclub manager. Moallic had operated La Louisiane restaurant in Paris, as well as prepared food at the Hong Kong Hilton and Café de Paris in Phnom Penh, Cambodia.

Bringing Moallic on board with the restaurant was a smart choice. When the French Café opened, it was the only French restaurant located between Chicago and San Francisco. The allure of an "authentic French chef" attracted the "Jet Set," according to the *Sun Newspapers*.

Moallic did not stay at the restaurant for long, though, and in March 1969, Chef Yves Menes replaced him. A French chef with equally impressive credentials, Menes came to Omaha by way of the Ritz-Carlton Hotel in Boston. Previously, he'd worked in Helsinki, Finland, and Paris.

The dining room of the French Café. *Courtesy Benjamin Rothe.*

Owner of M's Pub, Ron Samuelson, which opened a block west three years after the French Café, reflected on the decades of success for the French Café, saying, "It was places like that that made it seem so intoxicating. I don't think the Old Market would ever have been as successful without the French Café."

"Intoxicating" is an apt descriptor. It was nearly impossible for diners not to get swept up in the romantic ambiance the restaurant had created. When conversation slowed at the white linen–covered table, diners could gaze out at Old Market happenings through floor-to-ceiling windows. Or they could eye the oversized black-and-white photos from Europe that were wallpapered onto some of the walls. A glass wall divided the east bar from the dining room; brick walls, fresh flowers on tables and stained-glass accents completed the look.

The restaurant's success was due largely to the revitalization of the Old Market, which could not have happened without the French Café opening in the first place. Within a year of the restaurant opening, the area started to attract tourists. In 1969, the *Omaha World-Herald* described what was bringing in the out-of-towners: "Old Market has a French restaurant, movie house, poster shop, antique shop, two art galleries, a number of artist studios, dress shop, coffee house, candle factory and a place where, if you have something creative to sell, it'll be sold for you—and that's not the complete list."

Some complained that the area was too much like San Francisco's Haight-Asbury neighborhood, mainly because some of the youth hanging out in the area looked like hippies. It wasn't the hippies, though, frequenting the French Café.

ON THE MENU

While the atmosphere was attractive, the real draw to the restaurant remained the food. One item that was always a must-order was the French onion soup, served in a traditional pot. That soup, *la soupe a l'oignon gratinee*, was one dollar when Menes was chef.

The menu, written completely in French, had an extensive appetizer list and included *escargot de Bourgogne* for $2.25, house pâté with pistachios for $1.75 and mussels for $1.50. In the restaurant's early days, seafood and other entrées ranged in price from $4.00 for a steak tartare to $10.00 for chateaubriand garnished with vegetables. Most entrées were around $6.00, and among those dishes was the rack of lamb and veal cordon bleu.

A waiter at the French Café brings food to a table. *Courtesy Maggie Osterberg.*

There was a variety of desserts on the menu ranging from $0.85 to $2.50. The French Café served chocolate mousse, cherries jubilee, crème de menthe parfait and a cheese plate. The most expensive dessert item was the *crepes suzette*, which is a French dessert similar to a pancake topped with citrus juice and brandy and set aflame tableside.

The Line Between Classical and Modern French

In the summer of 1970, Chef Menes and employees took an extended vacation. As the story goes, the restaurant stayed open, and an interesting incident occurred. It was recounted in the *Omaha World-Herald*. While most customers leave a restaurant when they learn the menu has changed because everyone in the kitchen is gone, one group decided to stay. Mark Mercer and Nicholas Bonham-Carter, son and nephew, respectively, of Sam Mercer, were there to take their order. The group ordered some of everything plus a lot of wine. They liked it all so much that they stayed from 2:00 to 11:00 p.m. and ordered another round of "some of everything" before finally leaving.

In 1970, Tony Abbott and Michael Harrison joined the staff as managers. A year later, the two bought the restaurant from Mercer. Abbott stayed at the helm until the end, with the help of his wife, Valerie.

Abbott was admired by many for being able to reinvent the wheel from time to time. In 1979, the restaurant was honored in *Mainliner* magazine.

In an attempt to reinvent itself, in its last decade of operation, the restaurant's owners and staff tried to shake off the high-falutin' reputation and update some of the fading interior. Even with changes, it remained a restaurant for special occasions: anniversary dinners, graduation celebrations and birthdays. The Rothe family started a tradition of celebrating their mom's birthday every year on Christmas Eve at the restaurant. Ben Rothe recalled those meals starting in the mid-1990s and occurring annually until the final Christmas at the French Café in 2011.

In 2008, the chips in the façade did not escape the attention of one restaurant critic, who described it as "over-priced former glory showing its cracks." The *Omaha World-Herald* critic wrote:

> *Although still bejeweled with stained glass and wallpapered with those glorious, larger-than-life photos of European markets and cafes, the*

The romantic interior of the French Café. *Courtesy Maggie Osterberg.*

> *restaurant just seemed tired. There's a cozy sunken lounge opposite the bar, a windowed nook up front, and a more formal room in the rear with mirrored arches and the nude art that is a French restaurant's due. But the room most in use is the long dining room to the right. It had the feel of a house so long lived in that its inhabitants, still awash in some former splendor, don't notice its flaws.*

It wasn't all bad news in 2008. The creative food was still a huge draw. The reviewer noted some of the hits of her meals:

> *A pomegranate and black-pepper glazed rack of lamb with a dried cherry sauce that skillfully danced the border between sweet and savory. French onion soup with an amazing crispness to its broiled and bubbled Gruyere lid. A luscious and slightly spicy roasted red pepper sauce served with artfully plated crab cakes. Browned cubes of seasoned potato served with the omelet of the day. Tender chunks of beef and a savory bearnaise on the brunch brochette plate. And the classic crème brulee.*

It was around this time that Jeff Camp joined the kitchen staff. He had recently closed his restaurant Trovato's and, upon a friend's suggestion, took a sous chef position at the French Café. Three months later, the executive chef left, and Camp was promoted into the position.

His first order of business was to put his classical training to work, steering the staff back to classical preparation of dishes. Diners noticed the improvement. While the prices didn't change, customers began to understand dishes were worth the price. Camp said the clientele returned and the business was built back up.

However, while Camp's vision was to stay with classical French cuisine, he said the French Café's owner wanted to experiment with more modern food popularized by the growing trend of celebrity chefs. To that end, the owner hired a young chef de cuisine. Camp recalled the new chef's first night at the restaurant: "He went through the freezer to see what we had to work with. He was back there for two and a half hours. At the end of the service, I went in there to check on him. The guy had thrown away almost everything!" Camp explained that the new chef de cuisine didn't like frozen stuff, so he'd thrown out about $12,000 worth of perfectly good food. "Back then, you couldn't get everything fresh like you could now," Camp recalled.

Dining habits began to change and business began to slow down, even though the Old Market, now thriving, attracted more and more people,

The exterior of Le Bouillon. *Courtesy Kevin Reiner.*

locals and visitors. Finding parking became a constant frustration. Even with the crowds flocking to the area, they weren't coming in droves to the French Café.

The storied restaurant, the crown jewel of the Old Market, served its last meal on March 4, 2012.

Today, another French restaurant occupies the space: Le Bouillon, which is run by Chef Paul Kulik, who worked in the French Café in the 1990s.

Chapter 27

THE OMAHA DEPOT

Unique Architecture Was Not Enough to Keep a Restaurant Afloat

In the 1970s, railroad-themed restaurants were a trend popping up around the country. Many restaurants sprang up in abandoned railcars or depots renovated for a new purpose.

In Omaha, a California company brought its train concept in 1974 when it opened the Omaha Depot. Its location at 7775 Cass Street was nowhere near existing train tracks, so the firm had a unique structure built. Unfortunately, its depot structure and theme were not enough to keep its appeal for more than just a few years.

*****

Nothing like the Omaha Depot had ever been seen in Omaha before. The exterior of the building was designed to look like a train depot, and there were boxcars to complete the theme.

The Los Angeles firm California Specialties Company owned the chain. The firm opened locations throughout the Midwest in addition to its Cass Street location. Some speculate the firm opened too many locations too quickly. A year after opening the Omaha Depot, California Specialties Company closed several locations, including the Omaha location.

THE NEW OMAHA DEPOT

About a year following the Omaha Depot's closure, restaurant consultant Ken Franklin purchased the location, as well as two others, confident in his ability to run it much better. He told the *Omaha World-Herald* on April 1, 1977, that the new Omaha Depot wouldn't be too different from the old one. The only difference was that he'd add a ten-foot movie screen to show clips of classic films and comedies.

Franklin reopened the Omaha Depot and kept prices low, even for 1977 standards. The strip sirloin was the highest-priced menu item at $5.95. The restaurant had a large menu, including quiches, salads, omelets and the house specialties, zucchini bread, chip-fried potatoes and twice-baked potatoes.

Franklin was sure of the restaurant's success and waited to advertise until the restaurant was ready for a rush of new patrons. He said he'd learned from previous operations that inviting customers in before the personnel was ready was a recipe for disaster.

No ads have been found for the new and improved Omaha Depot. And it silently closed without a word. Jay Firmature, whose family purchased

The exterior of the Omaha Depot in 1974. The restaurant's building was designed to look like a train depot. *Courtesy the Durham Museum Photo Archive and* Omaha World-Herald.

the restaurant eight years after its demise, speculated in an *Omaha World-Herald* story that the size of the railcars might be one explanation for the Omaha Depot's demise. They were far too narrow for comfortable seating, according to Firmature.

Nothing appeared to have been removed after it closed in the 1970s, inviting break-ins for burglaries and vandalism. In a police report published in the *Omaha World-Herald* on April 27, 1978, the police caught two sets of teenage burglars the same night. Vandalism damages—some caused during previous break-ins—were estimated to be more than $10,000.

"The inside is a shambles. Ketchup has been poured all over, liquor emptied and windows, furniture and furnishings have been broken," Sergeant Paul Stone told the newspaper.

In 1983, the Firmature family purchased the Omaha Depot. The Firmatures were a well-known family of restaurateurs, and they set to renovating the building for a new restaurant. They began to remodel the structure, removing traces of most of the railroad theme. The railroad boxcars were sold to Skyline Woods Country Club. Renovations cost about $1 million.

The family opened the restaurant Firmature's in 1984. The new restaurant had a Victorian look inside and out. The restaurant closed soon after.

The Firmature family tried opening one more restaurant in the location, the Cheyenne Social Club. That venture closed in 1987. Eventually, the dance club Revolution and Sharky's took over the building.

In February 2000, it became the popular music venue the Music Box. It took $200,000 in renovations to make the building for the Music Box. Unusual for its time, the concert venue was smoke-free. In an interview with *Omaha World-Herald* following the opening weekend, the manager said even smokers thought the club was great. "Most people told me they didn't feel like they were in Omaha. They said they felt like they were out of town," said Meredith Partlow in the interview.

The first big act to play there was Tom Waits on March 18, 2000.

Financial struggles caused the Music Box to close in October 2003. The final inhabitant of the Omaha Depot building was Retro Metro. The building was demolished in March 2006 to make room for a 24 Hour Fitness location. Today, Genesis Health Clubs is located there.

Chapter 28

PALTANI'S FAMOUS TACOS AND MEXICAN FOODS

How a Mexican Restaurant with an Italian Name Became So Popular

One of Omaha's first Mexican restaurants had an Italian name. Its tacos were well known throughout the city, making the name forgivable.

Paltani's Famous Tacos and Mexican Foods began as a small lunch-only restaurant, eventually outgrowing its original location to fit the demand for its soft-shell tacos.

Before there was a Paltani's Famous Tacos and Mexican Foods, though, there was a Paltani's Lounge that opened in 1973. Owned by Paltani's Inc., it served primarily steaks and other grilled fare. Paltani's Inc. included Bernyce Paltani and sons Tom and Don. Don Paltani suggested they start serving some Mexican food at lunchtime, and it was the best thing to happen to the restaurant. At the time, Mexican food was exotic in Omaha. The last Paltani to manage the restaurant, Ed, said decades later at the announcement to close that it was the third Mexican restaurant to open in Omaha. The early days of Paltani's Famous Tacos and Mexican Foods are a bit fuzzy.

By 1983, the restaurant had grown its customer base enough to move to a larger location. The family-owned restaurant moved a mere couple blocks over to 4411 Center Street, where seating expanded to accommodate up to three hundred people, a number not including the party rooms. Previously, 4411 Center Street was home to North's Chuck Wagon, known for its buffet.

Paltani's Famous Tacos and Mexican Foods was not a fancy restaurant to impress but, rather, one that satisfied the diner without costing a fortune. Most entrées were served on paper plates.

There were two major draws to Paltani's: the prices, of course, and the tacos. While the menu was really only half Mexican cuisine, the tacos were by far the most popular thing to order. Prices for tacos in 1985 were $1.05 for bean, $1.25 for meat or turkey, $2.40 for a two-taco basket and $3.25 for a two-taco platter with rice and beans. These tacos were huge. They were served soft with a special sauce that few could replicate.

The rest of the menu was a variety of American and Italian dishes, including steaks, prime rib, perch, spaghetti and meatballs, barbecued ribs, liver and fried shrimp. They also served Rosie's special burrito, a burrito stuffed to near-bursting proportions, and Aunt Mary's homemade Italian sausage and pepper sandwich. Appetizers were a mix of Mexican flavors and Italian fare, from guacamole to toasted ravioli.

A cup of "very hot" Mexican chili was $1.50 and included two tortillas. Hamburgers were only $1.30. One of the most expensive items was the steak and lobster combo, which set a diner back by $9.95.

As popularity grew, the restaurant expanded to include side operations in the 1980s. Two fast-food versions of Paltani's opened—one at Crossroads Mall and the other in the Brandeis Building downtown.

One interesting promotion the Paltani family held in their main location occurred in 1986. They started giving away Iowa lottery tickets if anyone spent fifteen dollars or more at the restaurant. The promotion, surprisingly, didn't break any Nebraska laws.

FAREWELL TO PALTANI'S

Paltani's was still at its height when, in 1991, the sale of all Paltani's locations was announced. Ed Paltani, who was manager at the time, told the *Omaha World-Herald* that it came down to an offer no one could refuse. "The bottom line is money. And they just offered me more money than I thought we could make selling tacos."

An impromptu farewell party was held on December 31, 1990. On January 5, 1991, Paltani's served its last taco.

After Paltani's closed, the building and parking lot were purchased for future expansion of the Catholic Mutual Relief Society at 4223 Center Street. The plan at the time of the sale was to use the location as a parking lot for staff. When that didn't work out, the building was used by Catholic churches for bingo and receptions.

The two fast-food Paltani's locations were sold to Amigo's.

Chapter 29

BLUE FOX

Remembered for the Popular Greek Nights and Fine Seafood

In the late 1970s, a fine dining establishment with a seafood-dominated menu opened on the western side of Omaha. Critics said it wouldn't last; they thought Omahans wouldn't eat pricey seafood.

Co-owners George and Vivian Kokkalas proved critics wrong.

The Kokkalases opened Blue Fox at 1212 South 119th Street at the end of 1978. George, an immigrant who arrived in the United States from northern Greece in 1967, was the restaurant's executive chef. When the Kokkalases opened their restaurant, Vivian recalled everyone telling her the restaurant wouldn't last more than six months given the emphasis on seafood. But seafood was George's specialty, so that's the way it had to be. Years later, his passion for cuisine from his homeland became more prominent on the menu.

Even in landlocked Omaha, it was possible to get fresh fish and seafood, and George expertly knew how to prepare it with elegant flair and in large portions. Some of the dishes included orange roughy à la New Zealand or frog legs Provençal. One of the specialties was named after the Kokkalases' daughter, filet of sole "Ala Maria." It was king crab meat with shrimp in a wine and cream sauce. Beyond seafood, the menu included crisp roast duck, chicken Mediterranean, veal Madeira, rack of lamb and chateaubriand. Entrées came with a salad and choice of rice or potato of the day. One of the crowd-pleasing appetizers arrived at the table on fire: the *sanganaki*, a Balkan kasserie cheese with brandy set aflame.

Prices were kept pretty reasonable considering the extensive preparation some dishes required. In 1993, orange roughy was $9.95 and an eleven-ounce lobster tail was $25.00. Desserts were exquisite and included bananas Foster (for two, $7.95), peach Melba ($3.25) and chocolate mousse ($2.95).

THE WAIT STAFF–CUSTOMER RELATIONSHIP

One of the hallmarks of service at Blue Fox was the relationship between the wait staff and customers. Ten years after opening, many of the original waiter staff were still on board. In 1990, co-owner Vivian Kokkalas told the *Omaha World-Herald* that some of them had developed a following.

Since dining at Blue Fox was meant to be an experience, it was important not to rush customers through their meals. Customer service was key at the restaurant, and the waiters never imposed themselves on diners. To keep the experience feeling intimate—even in a spacious dining room—tables were spaced far apart, and candles lit individual tables.

The experience was so polished and reputable that Blue Fox became a popular spot for wedding proposals. The owners even saw some of those proposals return for their first anniversary dinner. It was also a spot for West Omaha prom dates.

GREEK ON THE MENU

In 1993, there were hints of a change at Blue Fox. The *Omaha World-Herald* restaurant critic remarked that there were Greek touches included in the menu, "and one gets the impression that this gifted chef would like to season his menu with more of it."

It was true. George began showcasing cuisine from his homeland in the early 1990s, first introducing Greek Nights to the restaurant. These special Greek Nights had live entertainment, and the menu was all Greek specialties. Greek Nights were popular, and with the lower prices for Greek food, they helped chip away at the image of an expensive, and a little old-fashioned, restaurant. They must have been profitable, too.

In November 1994, Blue Fox closed, and by December, George had reopened the restaurant as Georgio's, serving budget-friendly Greek cuisine. Georgio's had a slightly different look than Blue Fox. The new restaurant had been updated with white wallpaper and blue accents and an inviting bar.

Entrées—like *souvlaki*, skewered cubes of pork loin, and *spanakopita*, spinach and feta cheese wrapped in phyllo pastry—were all less than six dollars. A specialty menu in the evening had prices in the ten- to sixteen-dollar range. One of the restaurant's most popular dishes was the shrimp scorpio, which was linguine with shrimp, garlic, onions, feta cheese and tomato sauce. They served Greek wine, Greek beer and the Greek liqueur *ouzo*.

As Georgio's, the Kokkalases continued presenting Greek Nights at the restaurants, with live Greek music and sometimes a belly dancer.

Even with the popularity of those nights, the Greek restaurant didn't last long. Georgio's was sold to Louis Finocchiaro on April 26, 1996. By late summer, Finocchiaro had opened Thunderbird Grill, an upscale San Francisco grill. Thunderbird Grill had a range of low-cost hot sandwiches and dinner entrées ranging between ten and twenty dollars. The emphasis was on flavor and a visually colorful presentation. The chefs were Paul Sachs from M's Pub and an executive chef from Salt Lake City named Michael Osten.

A year later, the restaurant became Yo Yo Grill, a bistro-like restaurant owned by Mac Thompson, Bill Johnette and Gene Dunn. The most recent occupant of the space is Absolutely Fresh Seafood store, which added a restaurant, Shucks, in 2006. John Dye was the chef when the restaurant opened.

Chapter 30

MAXINE'S

Where Everyone Went for Omaha's Most Memorable Brunch

Maxine's doesn't fit as neatly into the Omaha dining landscape as the other mostly locally owned restaurants did. For one, it was a hotel chain restaurant. But what Maxine's succeeded at was integrating itself into the community. It adapted its menu to have more beef-centric entrées to better meet the expectations travelers had of Omaha. It created one of the most memorable Sunday brunches this city has ever seen. And so, for nearly twenty years, Maxine's was consistently ranked one of Omaha's best restaurants.

* * * * *

Before there was a Maxine's, there was the Beef Barron on the nineteenth floor of 1616 Dodge Street. Originally conceived as a sophisticated rotating restaurant in the Omaha Hilton, the western-themed restaurant ended up stationary due to budget restrictions, though it did have a rotating lounge at its center.

By 1980, the rotating lounge had been removed and a dance floor was put in place, and the Omaha Hilton was bought by the Red Lion hotel chain. The western-themed restaurant was changed, and Maxine's was introduced to Omaha. The hotel invested nearly $1 million to update the restaurant. More improvements came along in 1988, adding another $14 million in updates.

The Omaha Hilton exterior when Beef Baron Restaurant was on the nineteenth floor. *Courtesy Larry Richling.*

Maxine's Charm

From the start, Maxine's was able to boast a spectacular view when it opened on November 1, 1981. The renovations raised the floor two feet so every table could enjoy the view through the floor-to-ceiling windows. At night, guests could gaze toward downtown Omaha's twinkling lights. The decor was art deco influenced, with brown velvet-backed booths, carved wood on the walls and etched glass.

The menu was upscale and adjusted slightly from the chain's standards by adding more beef to the menu in order to meet out-of-towners' expectations of what dining in Nebraska entailed. The menu was expensive by Omaha standards. The price averaged about $10.00 per person in 1989. Brunch was even more. In 1993, brunch was $11.95 for adults and $6.95 for children. Entrées were upscale, with fancy-sounding names like lamb loin Wyoming finished in a rosemary pine nut sauce and Australian rock lobster tail.

The wait staff was trained to counter what some thought was a stuffy atmosphere, though surely the black tuxes and red bowties didn't help. The waiters would jovially converse with diners and explain the menu without a hint of attitude. One restaurant reviewer in 1989 admired the wait staff, saying, "Watching servers at work is like watching a well-choreographed ballet."

One of the restaurant's signature experiences was having a dish prepared tableside, including steak Diane and Caesar salad, as well as desserts like bananas Jamaican and cherries jubilee. The server would ladle brandy into a pan beneath it while blue flames danced up. With a flick of the wrist, the orange flames spring up in the pan around its contents, usually beef, crepes or ice cream. Diners edged back in their seats from the heat.

THE MAGNIFICENT BRUNCH

The most memorable experience at Maxine's had to be the Sunday brunch. In 1989, this huge weekly event attracted about 625 diners in a day. People knew to get there early or face a long wait. Mother's Day and Easter brunches were the restaurant's biggest days of the year. To accommodate the crowds on those holidays, the buffet was offered in the hotel's Grand Ballroom as well as in Maxine's.

The scene of Maxine's Sunday brunch was elegant. Each week, there were new ice sculptures carved by chef Pat Gallagher. Chefs worked both ends of the buffet line to serving up made-to-order breakfast staples like omelets.

The brunch menu was vast. Some of the offerings in one week included waffles; scrambled eggs; French toast; muffins, rolls, croissants, corn bread and other breads; bacon and sausage; biscuits and gravy; Cajun new potatoes; boned salmon; chilled shrimp; smoked salmon; fruits and salads; and cottage cheese. Rotating entrées included Parmesan chicken, seafood jambalaya with clams, sweet-and-sour chicken breast and roast baron of beef. And, of course, there was dessert. Some of the options, again in a single visit, included éclairs; strawberry, orange or chocolate cakes; ice cream sundaes; and cheesecake. Champagne and other wines were available after noon.

It was no wonder the brunch was a favorite. Officially, it was announced as a reader favorite in the *Omaha World-Herald* in 1991.

Certainly, the restaurant had its local fans. When surveying who was frequenting the restaurant, hotel management was surprised to see just how much the local community embraced the restaurant. In 1990, management discovered that 70 percent of diners were locals, not hotel guests.

A critic from the *Omaha World-Herald* explained the appeal in 1989: "Here is a truly elegant dining experience, not just a hotel meal, where you will feel more than comfortable on a special occasion, on a regular basis if you enjoy excellent treatment, on an impress-them-snooty-out-of-towners date."

CHANGES MARK A TURNING POINT

The Red Lion chain changed its restaurant format in 1993. Maxine's was not immune to the changes, and the new menu was put into effect. The food became lighter and emphasized freshness, white meat and fish entrées and using fresh vegetables and fruit in dishes. However, some of the staples like steak Diane and shrimp scampi remained on the menu.

There was also a push that year to make the restaurant more accessible to the average patron. Prices were lowered in an attempt to remove the assumption that the place was only for the well-heeled. The restaurant started an express lunch hour with meals for $6.95. Entrées were guaranteed to arrive at the table in fifteen minutes.

Following the new price change, dining room manager Arelen Ellis announced more news to the *Omaha World-Herald*: "Anyone can come here. There is no dress code requiring coat and tie, and we have converted our lounge to R.J. Grins, a place with its own personality. It's an activity bar now, with theme nights, including a country-western night on Tuesdays."

Not all the healthy changes stuck. In 1996, the restaurant added back some flambées with tableside preparation.

In 1997, DoubleTree bought the hotel, but Maxine's continued, along with its popular tableside preparation. However, the restaurant under the new DoubleTree management did not last much longer. The restaurant was closed on December 31, 1999. Doubletree general manager Mark Lauer explained to the *Omaha World-Herald* that "demographic changes in the city and competition from Iowa casinos had an impact on Maxine's."

The space was still used from time to time. Until 2003, the nineteenth floor was used for wedding rentals and other private parties. After that, it was remodeled to be used for conferences.

BIBLIOGRAPHY

Author's note: Writing this book could not have been possible without the reporting found in the *Omaha World-Herald*, *Omaha Daily Bee*, *Omaha Star*, *Plattsmouth Journal* and other newspaper and print publications like the *New York Times*, *Food & Spirits Omaha*, *NEBRASKA history* magazine and *Saveur* magazine, as well as the television station KCET.

Bristow, David L. *A Dirty, Wicked Town: Tales of 19th Century Omaha.* Caldwell, ID: Caxton Press, 2000.

CNBC. *Warren Buffett: The Billionaire Next Door—Going Global.* 2007.

Grace, Rachel P. *Omaha Food: Bigger Than Beef.* Charleston, SC: The History Press, 2015.

Holland, Matt. *Ahead of Their Time.* North Charleston, SC: CreateSpace Independent Publishing Platform, 2014.

The Junior League of Omaha. *Toast to Omaha: A Cookbook.* Omaha, NE: Quebecor Books, 2006.

Killian, Margaret Patricia. *Born Rich: A Historical Book of Omaha.* N.p.: Assistance League of Omaha, 1978.

Larsen, Lawrence H., and Barbara J. Cottrell. *The Gate City: A History of Omaha.* Boulder, CO: Pruett Publishing Company, 1982.

Larsen, Lawrence H., et al. *Upstream: An Urban Biography of Metropolis Omaha & Council Bluffs.* Lincoln: University of Nebraska Press, 2007.

Limprecht, Hollis J. *A Century of Service, 1885–1985.* Omaha, NE: Omaha World-Herald Company, 1985.

Mercer, Samuel. *The Old Market of Omaha*. Omaha, NE: Old Market Press, 1994.

Omaha World-Herald Company. *Omaha, Times Remembered!* N.p., 1999.

———. *Omaha, Times Remembered!* Volume III. N.p., 2002.

Otis, Harry B. *E Pluribus Omaha: Immigrants All*. Omaha, NE: Historical Society of Douglas County, 2000.

ABOUT THE AUTHOR

Kim Reiner lives in Omaha, Nebraska, with her husband, two children and her dog, Carl, who eats books. A former newspaper editor, Kim spends her free time freelance writing, blogging and eating a lot of good food at local restaurants. This is her first book.